ONE
MINUTE
DEVOTIONS

ONE THOUGHT. ONE SCRIPTURE. ONE PRAYER.

RICHARD EXLEY

WORD & SPIRIT
PUBLISHING
www.wordandspiritpublishing.com

16 15 14 13   10 9 8 7 6 5 4 3 2 1

One-Minute Devotions One Thought. One Scripture. One Prayer

ISBN: 978-1-936314-90-4

Published by Word & Spirit Publishing.

INTRODUCTION

When asked, "What is the one greatest obstacle you struggle with in your devotional life?" four out of five respondents said, "Time."

That's why I've written *One-Minute Devotions.* It's designed for the twenty-first century person who has too much to do and too little time to do it. In sixty seconds I will give you a life-changing spiritual thought, a relevant verse of scripture, and a sentence prayer that is refreshingly transparent. Whether you are a new Christ-follower or a mature believer, you will receive insights and inspiration to enrich your life.

As you prepare for the devotional life, it is important to approach it realistically. Nothing undermines determination faster than repeated failure. That's why it is so important to make a commitment you can keep no matter how small—even if it's only sixty seconds each morning. If you decided to take up running, you wouldn't begin with the Boston Marathon. You would probably start with a graduated training program, working up to longer distances over a period of time. Use that same principle for your devotional life.

Most of your devotional time will be discipline without immediate, measurable benefits. Don't let that discourage you. Consider the analogy of the runner again. Early in his training his running is pure drudgery, sometimes it is closer to sheer torture. His muscles get sore, his feet hurt, sometimes he gets blisters or shin splints; but over a period of weeks his body rounds into shape. Without realizing it, he starts to feel better. Even after he is in shape, there will be days when he has to force himself to run. As often as not the actual act of running is more discipline than pleasure.

So it is with the devotional life. The spiritual benefits are seldom immediately apparent. Sometimes after days, or even weeks, you feel no closer to the Lord. It seems you are making no progress. Don't give up. Like the runner, your spiritual man is slowly rounding into shape.

Marathoners talk of "breaking through the wall." They run until they are on the verge of collapsing. By sheer determination they press on, and suddenly they are through the wall. They get their second wind, but it's more than that. They experience an almost euphoric feeling, a runner's high. That experience corresponds with those moments in our devotional life when we are literally overwhelmed with the presence of God. It does not happen every time we pray or read the Scriptures, but when it does, it makes everything—all the discipline, all the solitude and sacrifice, all the hours of waiting—worthwhile.

With those thoughts in mind, I invite you to join me for one minute each day. Together we will still our hearts before the Lord in order to allow Him to speak into our lives. From time to time, you will feel that the day's thought, or verse, or even the prayer was written just for you—so clearly will it speak to your immediate situation. On those days you will find yourself returning to the one-minute devotion all day long, maybe all week long. As one reader wrote, "…one minute to read, but food for a week."

Thanks for joining me on this faith journey. Together we will become all God has called us to be.

—Richard Exley

ONE MINUTE DEVOTIONS

JANUARY 1

Having once been lost in a smothering fog while fishing in the Gulf of Alaska, I know the importance of a reliable compass. Therefore I choose to trust God's Word, even when disappointment and loss make it impossible for me to understand His ways. And like an unerring compass, His Word guides me safely through the fog of my pain and confusion.

Psalm 119:105
"Your word is a lamp to my feet and a light for my path."

Lord Jesus, may I ever hide Your Word in my heart against the day when disappointment and despair tempt me to lose my way. In Your holy name I pray. Amen.

ONE MINUTE DEVOTIONS

JANUARY 2

Are you haunted by past failures? Don't despair! So was Moses. So was Peter. So was Paul. Yet God redeemed their sinful mistakes and turned their failures into material for ministry. He will do the same for you. No matter how great your disappointment, God can turn your heartbreak into hope. Your past does not have to determine your destiny. God is making all things new.

Romans 8:28
"And we know that in all things God works for the good of those who love him, who have been called according to his purpose."

Lord Jesus, we've all made bad decisions, done things we are ashamed of, and we've all lived with regret. Yet we do not lose hope. Instead we give You our sinful failures, believing that You will redeem our mistakes and deliver us from our past. In Your holy name I pray. Amen.

ONE MINUTE DEVOTIONS

JANUARY 3

Has life been unkind to you? Have you been disappointed, even betrayed, by a trusted friend or a family member? Don't despair! God can take the very worst the enemy brings against us and use it for our eternal good if we will give it to Him. Name your disappointment, identify your hurt; now surrender it to the Father and ask Him to redeem it.

Genesis 50:19-20
"But Joseph said to them, '... You intended to harm me,
but God intended it for good to accomplish what is now
being done, the saving of many lives.'"

Lord Jesus, I choose to trust You with the wounds my soul
has suffered. Instead of becoming bitter I make peace
with my pain, I turn it into an ally instead of an enemy.
Redeem it; turn it into material for ministry. In Your holy
name I pray. Amen.

ONE MINUTE DEVOTIONS

JANUARY 4

Have you wounded a trusted friend or colleague? Do you even now grieve over the spiritual or emotional harm you caused them? Regret is not enough. Reconciliation requires something more. Have you sought their forgiveness? Have you made restitution? While God does not require us to make restitution in order to receive salvation, our long-term spiritual and emotional wholeness may very well depend upon it.

Matthew 5:23-24
"If...your brother has something against you, leave your gift there in front of the altar. First go and be reconciled to your brother; then come and offer your gift."

Lord Jesus, help me to do everything in my power to heal the hurts and repair the damage I have done in order to restore the broken relationships in my life. In Your holy name I pray. Amen.

ONE
MINUTE
DEVOTIONS

JANUARY 5

As you look back over your spiritual journey, it is probably the hard times you remember most clearly, at least
that is how it is for me. No one in their right mind seeks for
hard times, but having experienced them we recognize their
value and cherish their benefits. It is in the hard times that the
Lord reveals Himself in truly life-changing ways, howbeit His
presence is seldom easy to discern except in retrospect.

2

Corinthians 1:9-10
*"But this happened that we might not rely on ourselves,
but on God...He has delivered us from such a deadly peril, and he will deliver us. On him we have set our hope."*

Lord Jesus, be with me in the midst of the storm. Reveal
Yourself to me, no matter how dark the night, and in my
weakness may I find Your perfect strength. In Your holy
name I pray. Amen.

ONE MINUTE DEVOTIONS

JANUARY 6

Recently, I was asked why we invite Jesus to be present in our services. "Hasn't He promised to be in your midst any time two or three of you gather in His name?" I responded by explaining that the abiding presence of the Lord is always present (Matthew 28:20), but we are praying for His manifest presence (Acts 16:22-26). His abiding presence sustains us until His manifest presence delivers us!

Acts 4:31
"After they prayed, the place where they were meeting was shaken. And they were all filled with the Holy Spirit and spoke the word of God boldly."

Lord Jesus, I thank You for the promise of Your presence. Now manifest Your power that I may speak the word of God boldly. In Your holy name I pray. Amen.

ONE MINUTE DEVOTIONS

JANUARY 7

Are you struggling to hear God's voice? Be careful. If you strain to hear His voice, you will probably imagine you have heard Him when He has not spoken. Relax. Be still. The Father wants you to hear His voice even more than you want to hear it and He will make His will known to you. Of that you may be sure.

Job 33:14-15
"For God does speak – now one way, now another…In a dream, in a vision of the night, when deep sleep falls on men as they slumber in their beds."

Lord Jesus, give me ears to hear Your voice, a heart to receive Your Word, a will to obey Your command and faith to act. In Your holy name I pray. Amen.

ONE MINUTE DEVOTIONS

JANUARY 8

We've all made mistakes, some worse than others, but we dare not allow regret to paralyze us. Don't live in the past. Learn from it, but don't become its prisoner. A wise man once said that failure is a teacher, a harsh one perhaps, but the best. You can be discouraged by failure or you can learn from it. The choice is yours.

Proverbs 24:16
"For though a righteous man falls seven times, he rises again."

Lord Jesus, don't let me waste my failures. Let me learn from the past without becoming imprisoned by it. In Your holy name I pray. Amen.

ONE MINUTE DEVOTIONS

JANUARY 9

Are you at odds with a friend or colleague? Have you allowed an offense, real or imagined, to wound a relationship? If that is the case, do everything in your power to restore that relationship, for a broken relationship is like a pebble in your shoe. You may ignore it for a while, but in time it will cripple you.

Proverbs 18:19
"An offended brother is more unyielding than a fortified city, and disputes are like the barred gates of a citadel."

Lord Jesus, help me to swallow my pride and do whatever it takes to restore my broken relationships. In Your holy name I pray. Amen.

ONE MINUTE
DEVOTIONS

JANUARY 10

For thirteen years Joseph was a slave and/or a prisoner, but he prevailed because the Lord was with him. In prison he remembered his God-given dreams and they sustained him. Let Joseph be your example. No matter what you are facing, you can overcome if you don't lose heart. The Lord is with you and He will fulfill His purposes in your life.

Psalm 138:7-8
"Though I walk in the midst of trouble, you preserve my life... The LORD will fulfill his purpose for me; your love, O LORD, endures forever."

Lord Jesus, strengthen me in the hour of my trial. Give me the faith to persevere no matter how dark the night or how severe the storm. In Your holy name I pray. Amen.

ONE MINUTE
DEVOTIONS

JANUARY 11

Nothing is more important to a vibrant spiritual life than prayer. What breath is to our body, prayer is to our soul. In prayer we experience fellowship with the Father to nurture our soul, guidance to direct us, and anointing to accomplish our life's work. Prayer is the single most important spiritual discipline and the source of our strength.

Luke 18:1 KJV
"...Men ought always to pray, and not to faint."

Lord Jesus, teach me to pray. Teach me to wait in Your holy presence until I have received strength from on high. In Your holy name I pray. Amen.

ONE MINUTE DEVOTIONS

JANUARY 12

The essence of prayer is fellowship, communication, intimacy—the pure pleasure of God's presence. Intercession is critical and petition is vital but they pale in comparison to the heart of prayer, which is relationship with the Father.

Romans 8:15-16

"You received the Spirit of sonship. And by him we cry, 'Abba Father.' The Spirit himself testifies with our spirit that we are God's children."

Lord Jesus, I long to commune with You as friend with friend. Bind our hearts together until I am truly one with You. In Your holy name I pray. Amen.

ONE MINUTE DEVOTIONS

JANUARY 13

Isolation and solitude are not the same thing. They look alike—that is, both are characterized by aloneness—but they are not the same. When we choose to be alone, that is solitude, but when we are forced to be alone, that is isolation. Even then we can choose to make peace with our loneliness, thus transforming isolation into solitude. And in solitude—alone with the Lord—our spiritual and emotional energies are renewed.

Isaiah 40:31 KJV
"They that wait upon the Lord shall renew their strength."

Lord Jesus, teach me to embrace my loneliness, to turn my solitude into intimacy with You. In Your holy name I pray. Amen.

ONE MINUTE DEVOTIONS

JANUARY 14

Silence is not an enemy to be avoided, but a friend to be embraced. It is the language of the soul, the language of intimacy. God often speaks to us through silence. In silence He teaches us the deep mysteries of the Spirit, the things that can never be communicated with mere words.

1 Kings 19:12-13
"And after the fire came a gentle whisper. When Elijah heard it, he pulled his cloak over his face and went out and stood at the mouth of the cave."

Lord Jesus, silence is foreign to me, noise being such an integral part of my world. Teach me to turn off my iPod and cell phone and embrace the silence that I may truly hear Your voice. In Your holy name I pray. Amen.

ONE MINUTE
DEVOTIONS

JANUARY 15

Nothing is more dangerous than an unexamined life. Self-questioning is the water of God's grace that keeps the modeling clay of our lives from hardening into something rigid and unchanging. Learn to ask yourself, "Why am I feeling this way? What does this say about me? What is God trying to tell me?"

Psalm 139:23
"Search me, O God, and know my heart; test me and know my anxious thoughts."

Lord Jesus, help me to face the truth about myself that I might become the person You have called me to be. In Your holy name I pray. Amen.

ONE MINUTE DEVOTIONS

JANUARY 16

When we seek for life's deepest meaning and fulfillment in God and God alone, He allows us to experience joy in our work, our friends, and our families. Now these "things" no longer betray us, for they have ceased to be substitutes for God and have become the gifts of God.

Matthew 6:33
"But seek first his kingdom and his righteousness, and all these things will be given to you as well."

Lord Jesus, You are my only security, my only source of fulfillment. Help me to seek for my life's meaning in You and You alone. In Your holy name I pray. Amen.

ONE MINUTE DEVOTIONS

JANUARY 17

Do you sometimes feel that your life is out of control, that God is conspicuously absent, that you have been left alone to figure things out for yourself? God has not abandoned you, even if it seems He has. Experience has shown me that His great faithfulness is best seen in retrospect. It is only as we look back over our lives that we realize God was everpresent and that He had a plan even before we had a problem.

Exodus 33:13
"If you are pleased with me, teach me your ways so I may know you and continue to find favor with you."

Lord Jesus, forgive me for the times I doubt Your trustworthiness. In the heat of the moment I am tempted to look at my circumstances rather than Your promises. Help me to always focus on Your near presence. In Your holy name I pray. Amen.

ONE MINUTE

DEVOTIONS

JANUARY 18

God-centered thinking does not deny the reality of our present situation, but it does put things into eternal perspective. Seen in the light of God's awesome power and eternal faithfulness, the challenges we face no longer intimidate us. With God's help we will overcome. What at first appear to be obstacles will prove to be opportunities.

Isaiah 43:2-3
"When you pass through the waters, I will be with you; and when you pass through the rivers, they will not sweep over you. When you walk through the fire, you will not be burned; the flames will not set you ablaze. For I am the LORD, your God, the Holy One of Israel, your Savior."

Lord Jesus, help me to focus on You and Your sufficiency rather than on my circumstances. In Your Holy name I pray. Amen.

ONE
MINUTE
DEVOTIONS

JANUARY 19

What Jacob experienced the night that he wrestled with God, in the dark, on the muddy bank of the Jabbok, was true prayer—life-changing prayer. We used to have prayer meetings like that. "Praying through" we called it, which meant that we weren't leaving the place of prayer until God touched us, cleansed us, made us new! Like Jacob, we determined, "I will not let you go unless you bless me" (Genesis 32:26).

Hebrews 5:7
"During the days of Jesus' life on earth, he offered up prayers and petitions with fervent cries and tears to the one who could save him from death, and he was heard because of his reverent submission."

Lord Jesus, make my prayers passionate. Empower me to pray with tears and fervent cries even as I submit to Your will. In Your holy name I pray. Amen.

ONE MINUTE DEVOTIONS

JANUARY 20

The ultimate purpose of friendship is not account-ability but nurture. True friends hold each other accountable, to be sure. Yet if that becomes the primary function of the relationship, the friendship will not long survive. The bread that nourishes friendship is acceptance and communication, not accountability.

1 Samuel 23:16-17
"And Saul's son Jonathan went to David at Horesh and helped him find strength in God.... 'Don't be afraid,' he said. '...You will be king over Israel, and I will be second to you.'"

Lord Jesus, teach me to be a true friend who helps each others find strength in God. In Your holy name I pray. Amen.

ONE
MINUTE
DEVOTIONS

JANUARY 21

If you cannot talk about past hurts and betrayals without experiencing strong emotions, then you are probably still dealing with unforgiveness. When we have truly forgiven those who have sinned against us, we can remember the betrayal without reliving the pain.

Matthew 18:21-22
"Lord, how many times shall I forgive my brother when he sins against me? Up to seven times?' Jesus answered, 'I tell you, not seven times, but seventy-seven times.'"

Lord Jesus, by an act of my will I choose to forgive those who have sinned against me. Make my obedient act of faith real in my spirit and in my emotions. In Your holy name I pray. Amen.

ONE MINUTE
DEVOTIONS

JANUARY 22

Every relationship goes through periods of testing, times of boredom, times when those involved in the relationship must decide whether they are going to develop it to its fullest potential or slide off sideways and begin a new one. Developing a true friendship means digging deep. The stuff of which true friendship is made comes from the depth of our souls. Those who dare to make the commitment discover not only the treasure of a true friend, but the truth about themselves as well.

1 Samuel 18:1
"Jonathan became one in spirit with David, and he loved him as himself."

Lord Jesus, give me the strength to remain faithful no matter how severely my relationships are tested. In Your holy name I pray. Amen.

ONE MINUTE
DEVOTIONS

January 23

Loneliness is a universal human phenomenon. Sooner or later we all experience it. Just as the body expresses its need for food through hunger, so the soul expresses its need for relationships through feelings of loneliness. Relationships are to the soul what breath is to the body; without them we cannot truly experience life.

Ecclesiastes 4:9-10
"Two are better than one. …If one falls down, his friend can help him up. But pity the man who falls and has no one to help him up!"

Lord Jesus, don't let me wallow in my loneliness. Instead let it motivate me to reach out to others who may be just as lonely as I am. In Your holy name I pray. Amen.

ONE MINUTE DEVOTIONS

JANUARY 24

A true friend encourages you when you are struggling. He corrects you, gently and with love, when you have gone astray. He forgives you when you fail. He prods you to personal growth, stretches you to your full potential, and most amazing of all, he celebrates your successes as if they were his own.

Galatians 6:1-2
"If someone is caught in a sin, you who are spiritual should restore him gently....Carry each other's burdens, and in this way you will fulfill the law of Christ."

Lord Jesus, I thank You for the special friends who have celebrated my small successes as if they were their own and who have strengthened and encouraged me in the time of trouble. Bless them I pray in Jesus name. Amen.

ONE MINUTE DEVOTIONS

JANUARY 25

It's terribly painful to admit that the problem we face is our sinfulness. It's not circumstances, nor temperament, nor personality, not even the sinful thing we have done, but it is us—our sinfulness. Painful? Yes. But it is also good to have called it by its rightful name—sin—because having fearlessly owned our own sinfulness; we can now be forgiven and transformed.

1 John 1:8-10
"If we claim to be without sin, we deceive ourselves and the truth is not in us. If we confess our sins, he is faithful and just and will forgive us our sins and purify us from all unrighteousness."

Lord Jesus, I have no excuse, no self-justifying explanation. I am a sinner and You are my only hope. Forgive me and change me. In Your holy name I pray. Amen.

ONE MINUTE

DEVOTIONS

JANUARY 26

When we approach God with less than complete honesty, we become actors playing a role—what the Bible calls a hypocrite. As a consequence, we can have only the most superficial relationship with Him because the self we bring to the relationship is a false self. When we pretend to be something we are not, our spiritual life lacks vitality and our relationships are shallow and unfulfilling.

Jeremiah 17:9
"The heart is deceitful above all things and beyond cure. Who can understand it?"

Lord Jesus, wrestle with me in the dark night of my dishonesty until, like Jacob of old, I tell You who I really am. Force me to confess and claim my identity, believing such honest confession births the intimacy that makes me new. In Your holy name I pray. Amen.

ONE MINUTE DEVOTIONS

JANUARY 27

By trying to give our children everything—music lessons, ballet, drama classes, gymnastics, soccer, swimming, little league, ad infinitum—we end up depriving them of the thing they need most: time to be a child. Wouldn't it be better to teach our children how to choose what is most important to them? Learning to make value decisions at an early age will prepare them to make wise choices later in life.

Proverbs 22:6
"Train a child in the way he should go, and when he is old he will not turn from it."

Lord Jesus, help me to give my children spiritual values rather than cultural conformity that they may grow up to make wise decisions. In Your holy name I pray. Amen.

ONE MINUTE DEVOTIONS

JANUARY 28

A trysting place is where we meet with God. It may be a physical place like an empty sanctuary or a park bench, or it may be a state of mind and heart. When we lived in a cabin on Beaver Lake, my trysting place was a wooden rocker situated by the pot-bellied stove; now it's the small study in my home. Wherever your trysting place, it will be a place to which you retreat for spiritual renewal.

Psalm 26:8
"I love the house where you live, O Lord, the place where your glory dwells."

Lord Jesus, don't allow anything—not the pressing demands of my busy life or the clamoring of others—to keep me from our appointed time. In Your holy name I pray. Amen.

ONE MINUTE
DEVOTIONS

JANUARY 29

Never is the heart more deceitful than when we attempt to justify our sinful actions by citing the evil done by others, as if our transgressions will be excused because they are not as great as someone else's. God will not judge us based on what others have done, but by His holy law. And since we can never live up to God's righteous requirements, our only hope is to trust in the finished work of Jesus Christ—His sinless life, His sacrificial death, and His glorious resurrection.

2 Corinthians 5:21
"God made him who had no sin to be sin for us, so that in him we might become the righteousness of God."

Lord Jesus, You are my only hope and I thank You for being made sin for me that I might be made the righteousness of God. In Your holy name I pray. Amen.

ONE MINUTE DEVOTIONS

JANUARY 30

Prayer is multidimensional. It includes petition, confession, intercession, and praise, but its highest purpose is fellowship with the Father. In prayer we share our needs with God, but more importantly we spend time with the Father. Relationship takes precedence over everything else. Remember, the primary purpose of prayer is not petition but fellowship. It's about spending time with the Lord.

Psalm 42:1-2
"As the deer pants for streams of water, so my soul pants for you, O God. My soul thirsts for God, for the living God."

Lord Jesus, my heart hungers for You. Not for what You can do for me, but for You personally. I want to commune with You as friend with friend. I want to spend so much time with You that I become like You. Grant this I pray in Your holy name. Amen.

ONE
MINUTE
DEVOTIONS

JANUARY 31

Seen through the lens of our grief, God appears small and far away—like looking at Him through the wrong end of a telescope. The sacrifice of praise turns the telescope around. Now, God is near and a very present help. His nearness does not take our pain away, but it does give us strength to bear it and hope for tomorrow.

Psalm 42:11
"Why are you downcast, O my soul? Why so disturbed within me? Put your hope in God, for I will yet praise him, my Savior and my God."

Lord Jesus, You are an ever-present help, especially in the time of trouble. Give me grace to praise You at all times, especially when life's difficulties have rendered me mute. In Your holy name I pray. Amen.

ONE MINUTE DEVOTIONS

FEBRUARY 1

Years ago I heard a gifted Bible teacher say, "God allows some things to happen to us in order to do something in us so He can do something through us." At first I was offended. To my way of thinking, difficulties did not come from God. But upon further reflection I am convinced she was right. The key word here is "allows." Both Joseph of Old Testament fame and the apostle Paul are classic examples of how God uses the circumstances of our lives to further His eternal purposes.

Philippians 1:12
"Now I want you to know brothers, that what has happened to me has really served to advance the gospel."

Lord Jesus, give me the faith to believe that You can take whatever happens to me and use it to advance the gospel. In Your holy name I pray. Amen.

ONE MINUTE
DEVOTIONS

FEBRUARY 2

Examine your memories. Is your memory bank filled with positive, faith building experiences, or have you carefully kept a litany of painful memories? Since not all our memories are positive, we must sift through them, choosing which ones to keep and which ones to discard. For the most part, happy people have mastered the holy art of remembering good things. When the present is difficult or foreboding, they simply reach back and draw strength from the past.

1 Chronicles 16:11-12
"Look to the LORD and his strength…Remember the wonders he has done; his miracles and the judgments he pronounced."

Lord Jesus, help me to remember Your great faithfulness and to draw strength from it when present difficulties tempt me to despair. In Your holy name I pray. Amen.

ONE MINUTE

DEVOTIONS

FEBRUARY 3

Grief and regret are close kin, at least on an emotional level. They both produce melancholy feelings and a painful sadness. Beyond that they are not at all alike. Grief is a healing emotion that brings closure while regret is an unhealthy fixation on the past. Do your grief work but avoid regret like the plague.

Matthew 5:4
"Blessed are those who mourn, for they will be comforted."

Lord Jesus, help me to grieve without succumbing to regret. And in my grief may I find You near, providing hope for the future. In Your holy name I pray. Amen.

ONE
MINUTE
DEVOTIONS

FEBRUARY 4

Following the loss of their unborn child, Jim and Dolly grieved unspeakably, but even in their times of greatest sorrow they offered a sacrifice of praise. Because they had worshipped God faithfully in the sunshine of their lives, they were able to worship Him even in the darkest night. Jim wrote, "It was easy to praise Him in May when we were celebrating Dolly's pregnancy. But it is important to praise Him now as we grieve the loss of our unborn child."

Psalm 9:1,10
"I will praise you, O LORD, with all my heart...Those who know your name will trust in you, for you, LORD, have never forsaken those who seek you."

Lord Jesus, help me to worship You faithfully when things are going well so that I may know how to find You should tragedy suddenly befall me. In Your holy name I pray. Amen.

ONE
MINUTE
DEVOTIONS

FEBRUARY 5

Contrary to popular theology, Christianity does not make us immune to the vicissitudes and sufferings so common to this life, but it does empower us to live with meaning in the midst of all kinds of adversity. The real miracle of Christianity is that God redeems the worst life throws at us, using it to contribute to our ultimate Christlikeness.

Philippians 4:12
"I have learned the secret of being content in any and every situation."

Lord Jesus, teach me to trust You no matter how severe the storm. May I always find Your grace sufficient. In Your holy name I pray. Amen.

ONE MINUTE DEVOTIONS

FEBRUARY 6

Are you trapped in regret, unable to embrace the future because of past mistakes? You don't have to live that way. There is nothing to be gained by continually reliving your mistakes. God has forgiven you, so let them go. Remember the lessons you've learned, but put your mistakes behind you and get on with your life.

Psalm 25:7
"Remember not the sins of my youth and my rebellious ways; according to your love remember me, for you are good, O LORD."

Lord Jesus, help me to embrace Your mercy and grace and stop living in the past. May I always remember the painful lessons I've learned lest I make the same mistakes again. In Your holy name I pray. Amen.

ONE MINUTE DEVOTIONS

FEBRUARY 7

After examining my prayer life, I can only conclude that there seems to be little or no correlation between the spiritual and emotional intensity of my prayers and their effectiveness. In truth, the power of prayer rests not in the intensity with which we pray, but in the God to whom we pray.

Matthew 6:7-8
"When you pray, do not keep on babbling like pagans, for they think they will be heard because of their many words. Do not be like them, for your Father knows what you need before you ask him."

Lord Jesus, I dare not trust in my merit or the power of the prayers I pray, or I will surely fail. When I pray, help me to trust You and You alone. In Your holy name I pray. Amen.

ONE MINUTE DEVOTIONS

FEBRUARY 8

If you want to understand what it means to be a true friend, study the friendship Jonathan and David shared. They each preferred the other above themselves. The measure of Jonathan's commitment to David was his willingness to give up the throne that was rightfully his. The measure of David's commitment to Jonathan was his unwillingness to do anything to make the throne his own. They were each willing to lay down their life for the other.

Proverbs 17:17
"A friend loves at all times, and a brother is born for a time of adversity."

Lord Jesus, thank You for those friends who seek my good above their own and who celebrate my small successes as if they were their own. Make me a friend like that. In Your holy name I pray. Amen.

ONE MINUTE DEVOTIONS

FEBRUARY 9

Someone once said that 'if only' are the two saddest words in the human vocabulary. When asked to explain he replied, "'If only' focuses on past failures and sentences us to a lifetime of regret." He then suggested that we replace 'if only' with 'next time,' which turns our attention to the future and inspires us to try again. Next time I will be a better friend. Next time I will make better decisions. Next time…

Proverbs 24:16
"For though a righteous man falls seven times, he rises again."

Lord Jesus, thank You for never giving up on me. Teach me to focus on the future and help me to believe I can overcome because You have made me an overcomer. In Your holy name I pray. Amen.

ONE MINUTE
DEVOTIONS

FEBRUARY 10

Have you ever noticed that following the initial euphoria after a great victory there is often an emotional letdown? That's been my experience, and as a result, I am convinced our greatest joy is found in striving for God-given goals, even more than in obtaining them. So dare to dream big dreams, dare to attempt great things for God.

Proverbs 2:6,7
"The LORD gives wisdom…He holds victory in store for the upright."

Lord Jesus, help me to celebrate my achievements without becoming complacent. Enlarge my vision so I may go from victory to victory. In Your holy name I pray. Amen.

ONE MINUTE DEVOTIONS

FEBRUARY 11

Forgiving those who have wronged us is often a process rather than a single event. It involves at least five steps: 1) identify your feelings; 2) confess your feelings to God; 3) ask God to change your feelings; 4) pronounce forgiveness specifically; and 5) release your feelings. We act in faith believing that God will do in us what we cannot do ourselves.

Colossians 3:13
"Bear with each other and forgive whatever grievances you may have against one another. Forgive as the Lord forgave you."

Lord Jesus, give me the strength to forgive those who have wronged me. In Your holy name I pray. Amen.

ONE MINUTE
DEVOTIONS

FEBRUARY 12

Suffering is not a riddle to be solved, but a mystery to be entrusted to the wisdom of God. Trying to figure out why tragedy strikes one family while another family is spared is an exercise in futility. It's like a dog chasing his tail. Relief comes only when you surrender your situation to the Lord and trust Him to redeem it.

John 9:2-3
"'Rabbi, who sinned, this man or his parents, that he was born blind?' 'Neither this man nor his parents sinned,' said Jesus, 'but this happened so that the work of God might be displayed in his life.'"

Lord Jesus, I surrender my suffering to You asking only that the work of God be displayed in my life. In Your holy name I pray. Amen.

ONE MINUTE DEVOTIONS

FEBRUARY 13

Do you feel trapped? Are you facing a situation that you seem powerless to change? Don't despair—no matter how hopeless your situation seems. With God all things are possible. Accept what you cannot change. Surrender it to God. Place your destiny in His hands. Trust your future to Him and He will take care of you.

Psalm 138:7,8
"Though I walk in the midst of trouble, you preserve my life; you stretch out your hand against the anger of my foes, with your right hand you save me. The LORD will fulfill his purpose for me."

Lord Jesus, I surrender my situation to You, believing that You will take care of me. I know You have a plan for my life. Help me to trust You more. In Your holy name I pray. Amen.

ONE
MINUTE
DEVOTIONS

FEBRUARY 14

What Jesus did on Golgotha was not only the greatest demonstration of love the world has ever seen, but also the most daring act of faith! Having voluntarily laid aside every advantage of His divine nature (see Philippians 2:6-8), Jesus lived life by the same limitations we all face. That means what He understood about his death and resurrection He understood by faith alone.

John 15:13
"Greater love has no one than this, that he lay down his life for his friends."

Lord Jesus, I am totally blown away by Your outrageous love and extreme faith. Help me to respond in kind. In Your holy name I pray. Amen.

ONE MINUTE
DEVOTIONS

FEBRUARY 15

Do you feel your past has disqualified you for spiritual service? That's exactly how the enemy wants you to feel, but it's a lie. In truth, there is no sin God cannot forgive, no experience He cannot use if you will surrender it to Him, no personal failure He cannot redeem and transform into material for ministry.

1 Timothy 1:12-13
"I thank Christ Jesus our Lord, who has given me strength, that he considered me faithful, appointing me to his service. Even though I was once a blasphemer and a persecutor and a violent man...."

Lord Jesus, forgive my sins and redeem my past. Turn my sinful mistakes into material for ministry. In Your holy name I pray. Amen.

ONE MINUTE
DEVOTIONS

FEBRUARY 16

The overcoming life is a combination of divine deliverance and daily disciplines. God breaks the strongholds in our life, delivering us from bondage, but if we are going to live in freedom, we will have to faithfully practice the spiritual disciplines of prayer, study of the Word, worship, and fellowship.

Romans 8:2
"Through Christ Jesus the law of the Spirit of life set me free from the law of sin and death."

Lord Jesus, cast down every sinful stronghold and deliver me from bondage. Make me an overcomer. In Your holy name I pray. Amen.

ONE MINUTE
DEVOTIONS

FEBRUARY 17

Whether God saves us from our Gethsemane or allows us to walk the Via Dolorosa (literally the sorrowful way) our ultimate deliverance is assured. "Jesus said...'He who believes in me will live, even though he dies'" (John 11:25).

Romans 8:37
"No, in all these things we are more than conquerors through him who loved us."

Lord Jesus, Your unconditional love sustains me and Your near presence gives me the strength to live with meaning no matter how severe the trial. For this, I give You thanks. In Your holy name I pray. Amen.

ONE
MINUTE
DEVOTIONS

FEBRUARY 18

For all our rationalization we cannot excuse our sin. There is only one thing that will deliver us from this condemnation—the grace of the Lord Jesus Christ. If He does not condemn us, then who are we to condemn ourselves? If He has forgiven us, how dare we not forgive ourselves?

Romans 8:1
"Therefore, there is now no condemnation for those who are in Christ Jesus."

Lord Jesus, I am so tired of punishing myself. No matter how much I suffer, I cannot undo the things I have done. I know You have forgiven me. Help me to forgive myself. In Your holy name I pray. Amen.

ONE MINUTE

DEVOTIONS

FEBRUARY 19

Life on our fallen planet is seldom easy and it is often filled with circumstances that try the strongest faith. More often than not, it is these dark times that produce the most profound and enriching experiences. Your miracle may come as supernatural deliverance, or it may come as special grace enabling you to live with meaning in the midst of great difficulties.

2 Corinthians 12:10
"That is why, for Christ's sake, I delight in weaknesses, in insults, in hardships, in persecutions, in difficulties. For when I am weak, then I am strong."

Lord Jesus, I place my life in Your hands. Whether You deliver me or give me grace to endure to the end, I will trust You. In Your holy name I pray. Amen.

ONE MINUTE
DEVOTIONS

FEBRUARY 20

The key to living a contented life is to let the Lord "tune" your emotions until they are "pitched" to His perfect will. Let Him help you base your emotions on who He is—His immutable character, His faithfulness—rather than on your circumstances.

Colossians 3:2-3
"Set your minds on things above, not on earthly things. For you died, and your life is now hidden with Christ in God."

Lord Jesus, the difficulties I face often tempt me to despair. Help me to focus on Your sufficiency rather than on my problems. In Your holy name I pray. Amen.

ONE MINUTE DEVOTIONS

FEBRUARY 21

Are you tormented by the memory of your sinful failures, haunted by the damage your willful disobedience has done to others? Don't despair! No matter what you have done, God's grace is greater than your sin! Remember, God has a long history of turning life's rejects into men and women of eternal worth.

1 Timothy 1:13,14
"Even though I was once a blasphemer and a persecutor and a violent man, I was shown mercy....The grace of our Lord was poured out on me abundantly, along with the faith and love that are in Christ Jesus."

Lord Jesus, help me to trust Your grace that I might be free from the shame of my sin. In Your holy name I pray. Amen.

ONE MINUTE DEVOTIONS

FEBRUARY 22

Are you plagued by self-doubt and feelings of inferiority? Do you try to banish these feelings by working harder and achieving more? Unfortunately there is not enough success in the world to overcome our self-doubt. Only in God can we find our true identity and value as persons. His every word—not our accomplishments—defines us.

Romans 8:16-17
"The Spirit himself testifies with our spirit that we are God's children. Now if we are children, then we are heirs – heirs of God and co-heirs with Christ."

Lord Jesus, I choose to base my self-image on Your Word rather than my accomplishments. Help me to trust You more. In Your holy name I pray. Amen.

ONE MINUTE DEVOTIONS

FEBRUARY 23

Sometimes the tempter comes as a roaring lion seeking whom he may devour. At other times he comes as a thief to kill, steal, and destroy. But more often than not, he masquerades as an angel of light. His most subtle temptations are those that tempt us to meet a legitimate need in an inappropriate way.

Matthew 4:2-3
"After fasting forty days and forty nights, he was hungry. The tempter came to him and said, 'If you are the Son of God, tell these stones to become bread.'"

Lord Jesus, help me to recognize the tempter—whatever his disguise. Deliver me from his evil schemes. In Your holy name I pray. Amen.

ONE MINUTE DEVOTIONS

FEBRUARY 24

When our daughter remembers her childhood, it's not the "things" we gave her that come to mind, but the experiences we shared. I can only conclude that there is nothing you can give your children that will be more lasting or more deeply appreciated than the gift of yourself. Remember, a child spells love "T I M E."

2 Timothy 1:5
"I have been reminded of your sincere faith, which first lived in your grandmother Lois and in your mother Eunice and, I am persuaded, now lives in you also."

Lord Jesus, I thank You for parents who gave me the gift of themselves and their most holy faith. Help me to pass it on to my children and grandchildren. In Your holy name I pray. Amen.

ONE MINUTE DEVOTIONS

FEBRUARY 25

Take a minute and count your blessings. What came to mind? A nice home? A reliable car? A good job? Stylish clothes and good food? Those are blessings to be sure, but they pale in comparison to the blessing of family and friends. In that regard I am a rich man indeed, for I have been blessed with a loving family and a number of special friends.

Proverbs 21:21
"He who pursues righteousness and love finds life, prosperity and honor."

Lord Jesus, thank You for the gift of family and friends. Their love and graciousness have enriched my life beyond measure. In Your holy name I pray. Amen.

ONE MINUTE DEVOTIONS

FEBRUARY 26

At the root of every spiritual struggle, there are two forces at war: not so much good and evil, but God and self. If that is the case, then it must be equally true that there is only one temptation: the ever-present temptation to choose my will over God's will, my way over God's way.

Ephesians 5:15-16
"Be very careful, then, how you live – not as unwise but as wise, making the most of every opportunity, because the days are evil."

Lord Jesus, save me from myself. Left to myself, I will always mess things up. Teach me to choose Your way, Your will. In Your holy name I pray. Amen.

One Minute Devotions

February 27

The tempter wants us to believe that God is hard-hearted, that He is quick to judge and slow to forgive. Nothing could be further from the truth. No matter how miserably we have failed, no matter how far we might have fallen, He stands ready to forgive. In truth, God is more eager to forgive us than we are to be forgiven.

Lamentations 3:22-23 RSV
"The steadfast love of the LORD never ceases, his mercies never come to an end; they are new every morning."

Lord Jesus, help me to trust Your love and receive Your forgiveness no matter how often I have failed. In Your holy name I pray. Amen.

ONE MINUTE
DEVOTIONS

FEBRUARY 28

Special friends are rare indeed. I've heard them called "five-fingered friends" because in the course of a lifetime, a person can usually count his special friends on the fingers of one hand. Experience has taught me that the best way to make a special friend is to be one.

2 Corinthians 7:5-6
"For when we came into Macedonia, we had no rest, but we were harassed at every turn—conflicts on the outside, fears within. But God, who comforts the downcast, comforted us by the coming of Titus."

Lord Jesus, I started to pray "give me a friend like that," instead I pray "make me a special friend." In Your holy name I pray. Amen.

ONE MINUTE DEVOTIONS

MARCH 1

Sometimes the things we have suffered are too painful to remember so we repress them. Unfortunately, that which we repress is beyond the reach of God's grace, and thus it lives on to torment us and to undermine our relationships. It's only as we "own" our past and bring it to God that His grace can truly make us new.

John 4:29
"Come, see a man who told me everything I ever did. Could this be the Christ?"

Lord Jesus, show me the futility of pretending and protesting my innocence. Give me the courage to own my past, and in this owning up, let me find forgiveness and freedom. In Your holy name I pray. Amen.

ONE MINUTE
DEVOTIONS

MARCH 2

G od can only deliver us from the things we confess, and we can only confess those things that we have allowed the Holy Spirit to reveal to us. As long as we deny their existence or refuse to identify them specifically, we condemn ourselves to a self-made purgatory. Come clean with God and He will set you free.

John 8:32
"Then you will know the truth, and the truth will set you free."

Lord Jesus, give me the courage to face the things I have so long denied. Hear my confession and deliver me. In Your holy name I pray.

ONE MINUTE
DEVOTIONS

MARCH 3

Do you love God simply for self's sake, for what you can get out of it? Or do you love God for God's sake, because God is truly worthy to be worshiped and loved? Almost everyone initially comes to God for what they can get out of the relationship. Only as we grow in grace do we learn to love God for God's sake, because He is worthy to be loved.

1 John 4:19
"We love because he first loved us."

1 John 4:19

Lord Jesus, I truly want to love You just because You are worthy to be loved, but I fear that I love You for what I can get out of it. Purify my love and help me to love You more. In Your holy name I pray. Amen.

ONE MINUTE DEVOTIONS

MARCH 4

True righteousness manifests itself from the inside out. It is more than a mere behavioral change; it is the transformation of the inner man by the power of the Holy Spirit. Truly we are a new creation in Christ Jesus with new attitudes and new desires.

2 Corinthians 5:17-18
"Therefore, if anyone is in Christ, he is a new creation; the old has gone, the new has come. All this is from God...."

Lord Jesus change me from the inside out, make me born again. Conform me to Your very own image. In Your holy name I pray. Amen.

ONE MINUTE DEVOTIONS

MARCH 5

As a young man, I feared God was going to turn me into some kind of a dull saintly personality if I surrendered my life to Him. I couldn't have been more wrong. Sanctification does not stymie our talents or personality. On the contrary, it enables us to realize our full potential by freeing us from the self-destructive power of our carnal nature.

John 8:36
"So if the Son sets you free, you will be free indeed."

Lord Jesus, I surrender myself completely to You. Conform me to Your very own image. Make me the man You created me to be. In Your holy name I pray. Amen.

ONE MINUTE
DEVOTIONS

MARCH 6

If you are facing spiritual or emotional burnout, you probably don't need a power encounter. What you need is relationship—a gentle whisper assuring you of your value, of your place in God's Kingdom, a "still small voice" telling you of His love.

Matthew 11:28
"Come to me, all you who are weary and burdened, and I will give you rest."

Lord Jesus, I am praying for every person who is spiritually and emotionally exhausted by life's unrelenting demands. Be very near to them. Give them rest and restore their strength. In Your holy name I pray. Amen.

ONE MINUTE DEVOTIONS

MARCH 7

You can't be close friends with everyone. You simply do not have the time or emotional energy. No matter how much you would like to be friends with everyone, it's simply not possible. So what can you do? You can strive to be emotionally present, to be "real" each time you interact with a person. The gift of your presence will affirm their personhood.

Romans 12:15
"Rejoice with those who rejoice; mourn with those who mourn."

Lord Jesus, forgive my "all or nothing" thinking. Teach me to give what I can, when I can, and to trust You to use others to make up the difference. In Your holy name I pray. Amen.

ONE MINUTE DEVOTIONS

MARCH 8

We do not remember David as an adulterer and a murderer, but as a man after God's own heart. Why? Because no matter how grievously he sinned, he knew how to find forgiveness. He never blamed anyone but himself. And because he took responsibility for his sin, God was able to forgive and restore him.

Psalm 32:1
"Blessed is he whose transgressions are forgiven, whose sins are covered."

Lord Jesus, hear my confession and forgive my sins. Make me truly someone who, like David, has a heart for God. In Your holy name I pray. Amen.

ONE MINUTE
DEVOTIONS

MARCH 9

God always stands ready to forgive our sinful mistakes, but not even forgiveness can change the past. What's done is done. Forgiveness does, however, do something better. It changes us and it unlocks the future.

Psalm 32:5
"I acknowledged my sin to you and did not cover up my iniquity. I said, 'I will confess my transgressions to the LORD' – *and you forgave the guilt of my sin."*

Lord Jesus, forgive me. Cleanse me from all my sins and change me. Make me truly one of Your people. In Your holy name I pray. Amen.

ONE MINUTE DEVOTIONS

MARCH 10

Few things in life are more important than our choice of friends. They will influence our values, help shape our character, and determine to no little degree what we make of ourselves. Choose them wisely and they will prove to be an invaluable asset. By the same token, the wrong friends can cause you more grief than you can imagine.

Proverbs 13:20
"He who walks with the wise grows wise, but a companion of fools suffers harm."

Lord Jesus, give me a discerning spirit. Help me to choose my friends wisely. In Your holy name I pray. Amen.

ONE MINUTE DEVOTIONS

MARCH 11

The root cause of virtually all spiritual failure is disobedience in the little things. Over a period of time your spiritual strength is compromised and then when a crisis of temptation arises, you simply do not have the will to resist. To the undiscerning it may appear that you were brought down by that final crisis, but in reality, it was the dry rot of disobedience that did you in.

John 14:15
"If you love me, you will obey what I command."

Lord Jesus, teach me to be obedient in all things, both large and small, that I may have the strength to stand in the hour of temptation. In Your holy name I pray. Amen.

ONE MINUTE DEVOTIONS

MARCH 12

Your only defense against the lies of the deceiver is the truth of God's Word. Nothing else will sustain you in the hour of temptation. Not reason, or logic, or even conscience. These are no match for the evil one. God's Word is your only defense.

Psalm 119:9,11
"How can a young man keep his way pure? By living according to your word. I have hidden your word in my heart that I might not sin against you."

Lord Jesus, I love Your Word. I meditate on it all day long. Your statutes are my heritage forever; they are the joy of my heart. May Your Word keep me pure. In Your holy name I pray. Amen.

ONE MINUTE
DEVOTIONS

MARCH 13

It is not weakness that causes us to sin, but willfulness. Yet, even in our sin we are tempted to rationalize rather than repent, but we must not succumb. Rationalization is deadly and must be avoided at all cost. It is a lie we tell ourselves that leads to self-deception and self-deception leads to death. Only true repentance produces life.

Acts 17:30
"In the past God overlooked such ignorance, but now he commands all people everywhere to repent."

Lord Jesus, I repent of my stubborn willfulness. Forgive my sinful disobedience and turn me around. In Your holy name I pray. Amen.

ONE MINUTE
DEVOTIONS

MARCH 14

Truth telling is seldom easy, but it is the key that unlocks the door to spiritual victory. As long as we deny our struggles and pretend to be something we are not, we will never be free. The person who is trapped in secret sin lives a double life. He appears to be a godly man, a faithful husband and father, but in secret, he is something else entirely. Now it is not just his sin that traps him, but his reputation as well. By pretending to have it all together, he cuts himself off from the help he so desperately needs.

Psalm 32:3-4
When I kept silent, my bones wasted away through my groaning all day long. For day and night your hand was heavy on me; my strength was sapped as in the heat of summer.

Lord Jesus, pride tempts me to pretend I'm something I'm not. Deliver me, I pray, from my "spiritual reputation" so I can experience the freedom that comes through honest confession. In Your holy name I pray. Amen.

ONE MINUTE DEVOTIONS

MARCH 15

Years ago, I opened the door to Mom's room and found her kneeling in prayer. Her face was full of feeling as she poured out her heart to the Lord she so dearly loved. The intensity of her intercession humbled me, and I listened in awe as she bombarded heaven on behalf of her children, grandchildren, and great-grandchildren. Who, I wondered, will pray for us when she is gone?

Proverbs 31:28,31
"Her children arise and call her blessed…Give her the reward she has earned, and let her works bring her praise at the city gate."

Lord Jesus, I thank You for godly mothers whose prayers have shaped their children and protected them. Bless them Lord and give them their reward. In Your holy name I pray. Amen.

ONE MINUTE DEVOTIONS

MARCH 16

Without Christ we are all faceless people, lacking distinction and detail. But when we turn to Him, He covers the canvas of our lives with the bright colors and intricate details of abundant life. He touches our mistakes, even our sins, with His grace and they become part of the finished product—a portrait of love.

Psalm 51:2,10
"Wash away all my iniquity and cleanse me from my sin. Create in me a pure heart, O God, and renew a steadfast spirit within me."

Lord Jesus, fill the flat emptiness of my life with the colors and details of Your choosing. Let the finished me be more Yours than mine. In Your holy name I pray. Amen.

ONE MINUTE DEVOTIONS

MARCH 17

Even as we celebrate the joys of life, there is another part of us that grieves for those who suffer. It is this spiritual sorrow that is our rite of passage into ministry. Thus it was with Jesus. His experience teaches us that it is not only possible to experience joy and sorrow simultaneously, but that it is mandatory if we are to live as authentic human beings.

Isaiah 53:3
"He was...a man of sorrows, and familiar with suffering."

Lord Jesus, teach me to live experiencing both joy and sorrow so I can be emotionally present in each ministry encounter. In Your holy name I pray. Amen.

ONE MINUTE
DEVOTIONS

MARCH 18

Good intentions are not enough. Our relationship to the poor must be guided not only by compassion, but also by Scripture. When we give people a handout rather than a hand up, we create dependency and a sense of entitlement. Rather than helping them achieve personal independence, we have locked them into a cycle of poverty.

Leviticus 23:22
"When you reap the harvest of your land, do not reap to the very edges of your field...Leave them for the poor and the alien."

Lord Jesus, grant me both wisdom and compassion that I may help the less fortunate without belittling them. In Your holy name I pray. Amen.

ONE MINUTE DEVOTIONS

MARCH 19

Mother has been gone several years now, but I remember her last days as if they just happened. While maintaining my vigil beside her hospital bed, I realized I had a choice. I could focus on this tragedy and Mother's impending death, or I could revisit the memories of the rich life she so freely shared with those she loved. I chose the latter and thus began a journey that gave birth to an overwhelming sense of gratitude that comforts me to this day.

Proverbs 31:29
"Many women do noble things, but you surpass them all."

Lord Jesus, help me to be grateful for all I've had rather than grieving over what I've lost. In Your holy name I pray. Amen.

ONE MINUTE
DEVOTIONS

MARCH 20

When you take a child fishing or to a ball game, it's not about the event, it's about building relationships and making memories. There will be plenty of time for fishing or playing golf when the children are grown and gone, but today is the only chance you will have to make this memory—a memory they will cherish for a lifetime.

Ephesians 6:4
"Fathers, do not exasperate your children; instead, bring them up in the training and instruction of the Lord."

Lord Jesus, thank You for the gift of children. Grant me patience and wisdom. Make me the parent You have called me to be. In Your holy name I pray. Amen.

ONE MINUTE
DEVOTIONS

MARCH 21

The longer I live, the more I realize just how blessed I have been. In addition to a very positive relationship with my parents and siblings, I was blessed with an extended family of loving grandparents, aunts, and uncles. As a result, I never doubted my worth as a person. Within the extended family circle I knew I had a place. I was loved. I was somebody.

Proverbs 3:1-2
"My son, do not forget my teaching, but keep my commands in your heart, for they will prolong your life many years and bring you prosperity."

Lord Jesus, thank You for the gift of family and the loving support they have provided. In Your holy name I pray. Amen.

ONE MINUTE DEVOTIONS

MARCH 22

Grandma Miller has been dead for nearly fifty years now, but she lives on in my memory and her influence shapes me still. She was tenacious, and from her example I learned to "hang tough" and finish what I started. She believed in me and taught me to believe in myself. I am who I am today, at least in part, because of the investment she made in me.

2 Timothy 1:5
"I have been reminded of your sincere faith, which first lived in your grandmother Lois and in your mother Eunice and, I am persuaded, now lives in you also."

Lord Jesus, I want to thank You for my godly heritage. Help me to pass it on to my children and grandchildren. In Your holy name I pray. Amen.

ONE MINUTE DEVOTIONS

MARCH 23

Don't confuse rashness with boldness. Rashness is recklessness without reason. Boldness, on the other hand, is a calculated risk based on the best possible information. While bold decisions don't always pan out, bold thinkers invariably win the day, so dare to do bold things for God.

Joshua 1:9
"Do not be terrified; do not be discouraged, for the LORD your God will be with you wherever you go."

Lord Jesus, help me to be a bold thinker willing to do daring things in Your service. In Your holy name I pray. Amen.

MARCH 24

No one goes through life unscathed. Sooner or later someone you trust will betray you, a business deal will go south leaving you in a financial crisis, illness will strike, or someone you love will die. When you have been wounded, it is critical to make peace with your pain, to turn it into an ally. Embrace it and learn from it. Remember, God has a long history of turning life's tragedies into opportunities for personal growth and development.

Romans 5:3-5
"We also rejoice in our sufferings, because we know that suffering produces perseverance; perseverance, character; and character, hope. And hope does not disappoint us, because God has poured out his love into our hearts by the Holy Spirit, whom he has given us."

Lord Jesus, help me to make peace with my pain, to turn it into an ally instead of an enemy so the works of God may be displayed in my life. In Your holy name I pray. Amen.

ONE MINUTE
DEVOTIONS

MARCH 25

God never gives us grace in advance. It always comes just when we need it. That's why people often say, "I could never bear something like that." Yet when it comes, they not only bear it but they do so with remarkable grace. Truly God's grace is sufficient, but it does not make things easy, just possible.

2 Corinthians 12:9
"But he said to me, 'My grace is sufficient for you, for my power is made perfect in weakness.'"

Lord Jesus, help me to live one day at a time, trusting in Your grace minute by minute. In Your holy name I pray. Amen.

ONE MINUTE DEVOTIONS

MARCH 26

Most of my life is behind me now and I find myself introspective from time to time. Do I have any regrets? A few. I wish I had been less full of myself. I wish I had invited people to receive Jesus every time I preached. I wish I had prayed for my family more faithfully. I wish I had been a better friend. I wish I had been a more godly man. Yet I'm thankful too, especially for God's amazing grace.

Philippians 4:4,6-7
"Rejoice in the Lord always....Do not be anxious about anything, but in everything, by prayer and petition, with thanksgiving, present your requests to God. And the peace of God, which transcends all understanding, will guard your hearts and your minds in Christ Jesus."

Lord Jesus, teach me to trust You more. In Your holy name I pray. Amen.

ONE MINUTE
DEVOTIONS

MARCH 27

Have you given up on your God-given dreams? You may feel that you simply do not have the wherewithal to see them become reality or you may feel that your willful disobedience has disqualified you. Either way, you will be tempted to give up. Don't! Instead, look to God. For He is the author and finisher of our faith, and He who began this good work in you will be faithful to bring it to completion.

Galatians 6:9 KJV
"Let us not be weary in well doing: for in due season we shall reap, if we faint not."

Lord Jesus, give me the strength to persevere so You can fulfill Your purposes in my life. In Your holy name I pray. Amen.

ONE MINUTE DEVOTIONS

MARCH 28

The images of the last days I spent with my father have been forever etched upon my heart. I will never forget the love and devotion heaped upon him by his family and friends. It was a rare and special thing and I can only conclude that the man or woman who goes into eternity loved like that is rich indeed.

Acts 20:37-38
"They all wept as they embraced him and kissed him. What grieved them the most was his statement that they would never see his face again."

Lord Jesus, help me to live selflessly and to die a beloved man. In Your holy name I pray. Amen.

ONE MINUTE DEVOTIONS

MARCH 29

I don't like to think of myself as a materialistic person, but driving away from the Highway 12 East storage complex, I could hardly come to any other conclusion. For nine years, I paid $37 a month to store things I hadn't used in nearly a decade. Add it up—nine years at $444 a year comes to $3,996. Now that's hardly what I would call good stewardship.

Luke 12:15
"Then he [Jesus] said to them, 'Watch out! Be on your guard against all kinds of greed; a man's life does not consist in the abundance of his possessions.'"

Lord Jesus, save me from greed before I drown in all this stuff. In Your holy name I pray. Amen.

ONE MINUTE
DEVOTIONS

MARCH 30

I suspect that many of you are in the same place I am—your plate is too full and as a result, life has lost its zest. It's time to take control of your life! Make a list of all of your responsibilities. Now decide what to delegate and what to let go undone. Finally, focus on those things only you can do—you are the only husband/wife your spouse has. You are the only father/mother your children have. You are....

Ecclesiastes 7:18
"The man who fears God will avoid all extremes."

Lord Jesus, forgive me for trying to do it all. I think I am being responsible but in reality, it's pride that drives me. Forgive me for acting as though I am indispensable. In Your Holy name I pray. Amen.

ONE MINUTE DEVOTIONS

MARCH 31

Have you filled your life with the urgent instead of the important, the good instead of the best, the insignificant instead of the eternal? If so, it's time to make some changes. Reordering your life won't be easy. People may misunderstand and that can be painful, but you can't allow the expectations of others to shape your life; not if you want to please God rather than man.

Ecclesiastes 12:13
"Fear God and keep his commandments, for this is the whole duty of man."

Lord Jesus, give me a discerning heart that I may order my steps according to Your ways. In Your holy name I pray. Amen.

ONE MINUTE
DEVOTIONS

APRIL 1

Most abusers were victims before they became perpetrators. Because they could not or would not make peace with their past, they condemned themselves to repeat it. Unless you choose to forgive those who have wronged you, you too will become the very thing you hate. But you don't have to repeat the past. With God's help, you can break the cycle of betrayal, make peace with your past, and forgive those who have wronged you.

Mark 5:15
"They saw the man who had been possessed by the legion of demons, sitting there, dressed and in his right mind."

Lord Jesus, heal my brokenness and set me free from the past. In Your holy name I pray. Amen.

ONE MINUTE
DEVOTIONS

APRIL 2

I'm ashamed to admit that my greatest temptation has been pride. Considering how modest my achievements have been, you may find that hard to believe. Experience, however, has taught me that success has only a small part to play in a person's susceptibility. What makes pride so deadly is the fact that we are usually blind to it. We can spot it in a heartbeat in others but not in ourselves—at least that's the way it is for me.

Proverbs 16:18
"Pride goes before destruction, a haughty spirit before a fall."

Lord Jesus, nothing is more dangerous than an out-of-control ego. Deliver me from fleshly pride and help me to walk humbly before You. In Your holy name I pray. Amen.

ONE MINUTE DEVOTIONS

APRIL 3

In *God, Man, and Archie Bunker,* Spencer Marsh begins the first sentence of the first chapter, "In the beginning Archie created God in his own image." Upon first reading, I found his statement clever and attention grabbing. Upon further reflection, I find it both profound and prophetic—an apt description of our postmodern culture with its freewheeling spirituality. What many believe about God is based on personal "spiritual" experience rather than on the revelation of Scripture.

2 Peter 1:16
"We did not follow cleverly invented stories when we told you about the power and coming of our Lord Jesus Christ."

Lord Jesus, help me to become a critical thinker without being a critical person. In Your holy name I pray. Amen.

ONE MINUTE
DEVOTIONS

APRIL 4

When it comes to divine healing there are no easy answers. Faith is a factor, but not the only factor, and not necessarily the deciding factor. I have witnessed enough supernatural healings to never lose hope, no matter how desperate the situation. Yet, I've preached enough funerals that I dare not be presumptuous. Christ has defeated death but He has not yet destroyed it and until He does, we will have to contend with both disease and death.

1 Corinthians 15:25-26
"For he must reign until he has put all his enemies under his feet. The last enemy to be destroyed is death."

Lord Jesus, You are the healer and I will trust You for my healing, whether in this life or the next. In Your holy name I pray. Amen.

ONE MINUTE DEVOTIONS

APRIL 5

The way to know God is relationally, the way a child knows his parents. The family is not an abstraction to be studied, but a community into which we are born. We know our parents because we are in relationship with them —we live in their home, we eat at their table. There are family rules to be sure, but we never mistake the rules for our parents. Spiritual truth is experienced through relationship with God. It comes to the heart first, then to the intellect.

John 3:3
"Jesus declared, 'I tell you the truth, no one can see the kingdom of God unless he is born again.'"

Lord Jesus, thank You for making it possible for me to be born again into the family of God, that I might truly know You. In Your holy name I pray. Amen.

ONE MINUTE
DEVOTIONS

APRIL 6

A friend was falsely accused. As a result, he lost his job and suffered some serious health issues. Through it all his heart remained pure. Not once did he speak disparagingly of those who had engineered his demise. Over coffee one morning, I asked him how he managed to keep such a positive outlook. Without a moment's hesitation he replied, "I've never been a bitter or vindictive person and I'm not going to allow anyone to make me into something I'm not."

1 Peter 2:15
"For it is God's will that by doing good you should silence the ignorant talk of foolish men."

Lord Jesus, help me to overcome evil with good and always manifest a Christ-like spirit. In Your holy name I pray. Amen.

One Minute Devotions

April 7

In these tumultuous times we must guard our hearts. We cannot allow heated political differences, financial crises, or hard times to turn us into angry or bitter people. We are called to love not only those who love us but also our enemies. Determine that with God's help you are going to respond in the Spirit of Christ, no matter what others do. Never allow anyone or any situation to make you into someone you are not.

⬡

Proverbs 4:23
"Above all else, guard your heart, for it is the wellspring of life."

⬡

Lord Jesus, give me a pure heart and a right spirit no matter what others may do. In Your holy name I pray. Amen.

ONE MINUTE DEVOTIONS

APRIL 8

We are called to stand for truth regardless of the cost, but we must always walk humbly and in love. In the past we have spoken truth but without love. As a result, we have been perceived as judgmental. Now some believers refuse to address the issues at all lest they be perceived as intolerant. Both extremes miss the mark. Truth without love is harsh and judgmental, even as love without truth is permissive. But when we speak the truth in love, it is transformational.

1 Peter 4:8
"Above all, love each other deeply, because love covers over a multitude of sins."

Lord Jesus, help me to speak the truth without being harsh and to show love without being permissive. In Your holy name I pray. Amen.

ONE MINUTE DEVOTIONS

APRIL 9

No one goes through this life unscathed. Sooner or later, tragedy will strike. When it does, lean on your friends. There may not be anything they can do to put your broken world back together. Nonetheless, their emotional support will be enormously valuable. Their prayers will be a source of great comfort, enabling you to bear things you never imagined yourself capable of bearing. And in the end, you will overcome.

Matthew 26:37-38
"He took Peter and the two sons of Zebedee along with him, and he began to be sorrowful and troubled. Then he said to them, 'My soul is overwhelmed with sorrow to the point of death. Stay here and keep watch with me.'"

Lord Jesus, help me to invest in my friends now so they will be there for me in the hour of my tribulation. In Your holy name I pray. Amen.

One Minute Devotions

APRIL 10

When your world is crumbling around you, run to Father God and throw yourself into His arms. Let Him hold you and comfort you. Meditate on what it means for Him to be your Father. Being a father myself, I know the feelings a father has for his children. Whatever touches my child touches me. If I, a mere mortal, have these kinds of feelings for my daughter, then I can only imagine how much more Father God cares for us, His children.

Psalm 103:13 NKJV
"As a father pities his children, so the LORD pities those who fear Him."

Heavenly Father, take me in Your arms and comfort me. Still my trembling heart and quiet my troubled soul. In the name of Jesus Christ I pray. Amen.

ONE MINUTE
DEVOTIONS

APRIL 11

When my grandson was just a little guy, he was always hurting himself. But instead of running to us for comfort, he would run away. If we tried to comfort him, he would strike out at us screaming, "Don't touch me. Leave me alone!" Although we were not responsible for his pain, he blamed us and would not allow us to comfort him. I cannot help thinking how like him we are. Let life deal us a crushing blow and we are quick to blame God.

Isaiah 41:13
"I am the LORD, your God, who takes hold of your right hand and says to you, Do not fear; I will help you."

Father God, forgive me for blaming You when tragedy strikes. Teach me to trust You at all times, but especially in the time of trouble. In the name of Jesus Christ I pray. Amen.

ONE MINUTE DEVOTIONS

APRIL 12

Is it hard for you to appreciate your achievements? Are you haunted with the thought that if others knew the whole truth about you, they would know what a phony you are? Are your bright and shining moments tainted with the shame of past sins or the pain of some unspeakable tragedy? If that's how you feel, it's time to receive God's forgiveness and make peace with your past.

Psalm 103:10,12
"He does not treat us as our sins deserve or repay us according to our iniquities. As far as the east is from the west, so far has he removed our transgressions from us."

Lord Jesus, help me to forgive myself because You have forgiven me. Help me celebrate my achievements without shame. In Your holy name I pray. Amen.

ONE
MINUTE
DEVOTIONS

APRIL 13

The real question isn't, "What's the worst thing that's ever happened to you?" but "What will you do?" Will you trust the Lord to heal your hurts, to redeem your troubles, and to fulfill His purposes in your life, or will you take matters into your own hands? How you answer that question is critically important, for it will determine both your spiritual and emotional wholeness as well as your destiny—so choose wisely.

1 Peter 5:10
"And the God of all grace, who called you to his eternal glory in Christ, after you have suffered a little while, will himself restore you and make you strong, firm and steadfast."

Lord Jesus, I bring You my hurts and disappointments believing You can redeem all the bad things that have happened to me. In Your holy name I pray. Amen.

ONE MINUTE
DEVOTIONS

APRIL 14

The first step in developing a meaningful devotional life is to find a good model. There are probably any number of godly men and women who could fill this role, but no one is more qualified than the Lord Jesus himself. Both the purity of His personal life and the power of His ministry flowed out of His relationship with the Father. And the quality of His relationship with the Father was a product of His spiritual disciplines—what we refer to as our devotional life.

Hebrews 10:22,23
"Let us draw near to God with a sincere heart in full assurance of faith…for he who promised is faithful."

Lord Jesus, You modeled the devotional life for me. Now empower me that I might follow in Your steps. In Your holy name I pray. Amen.

ONE
MINUTE
DEVOTIONS

APRIL 15

When the doctors informed us that Dad's death was imminent, my sister took a leave of absence from her job in order to help Mother care for him. Being the only daughter, she and Dad had a special relationship, making acceptance of his impending death especially difficult for her. Still, she served without flinching. Although her heart was breaking, she never complained. She performed even the most menial task with a grace that transformed it into an act of love. Her tireless efforts made Dad's last days not only bearable, but blessed.

Philippians 4:18
"They are a fragrant offering, an acceptable sacrifice, pleasing to God."

Lord Jesus, may this example inspire me to sacrificially serve those I love. In Your holy name I pray. Amen.

ONE MINUTE DEVOTIONS

APRIL 16

When compliments come my way, I'm always careful to pass them on to the One to whom all glory belongs. It's a discipline I learned from the late Corrie ten Boom. When she received a compliment she would say, "Thank you. I'll put that in my bouquet." When asked to explain she would say, "I think of every compliment as a flower. At the end of the day I arrange them into a bouquet and present them to Jesus."

John 12:3
"Then Mary took…an expensive perfume; she poured it on Jesus' feet and wiped his feet with her hair. And the house was filled with the fragrance of the perfume."

Lord Jesus, all glory and honor belong to You. Whatever awards or honors come my way I lay at Your feet. Receive my gift of worship. In Your holy name I pray. Amen.

ONE MINUTE
DEVOTIONS

APRIL 17

I still grieve over some of the mistakes I made when I was a young man, but I know I am forgiven and you can be too. No matter what you have done, God's grace is greater than your sin! John said, "If we confess our sins, he is faithful and just and will forgive us our sins and purify us from all unrighteousness" (1 John 1:9). The worst thing you can ever do is refuse God's grace and mercy.

Psalm 25:7
"Remember not the sins of my youth and my rebellious ways; according to your love remember me, for you are good, O Lord."

Lord Jesus, thank You for Your mercy and grace that makes all things new. In Your holy name I pray. Amen.

ONE MINUTE DEVOTIONS

APRIL 18

When I think of blind spots, I'm reminded of the medieval nobleman who built a castle that included a beautiful chapel where he often retired for prayer and meditation. Not infrequently, his prayers were interrupted by the screams of his enemies who were being tortured in the dungeon he had constructed directly beneath the chapel. Apparently, he saw nothing incongruent about praying while his enemies were being tortured and put to death. Which just goes to show that we all have blind spots—inconsistencies that are readily apparent to others, but that escape our notice.

Psalm 139:23,24
"Search me, O God, and know my heart;…See if there is any offensive way in me."

Lord Jesus, reveal my blind spots and inconsistencies that I may confess them and receive forgiveness. In Your holy name I pray. Amen.

ONE MINUTE
DEVOTIONS

APRIL 19

Sometimes good people make poor choices that result in unintended consequences. Maybe you've done that; I know I have. You may be living with the unintended consequences of a poor choice you made years ago. Try as you might, you cannot forgive yourself or move on with your life. I bring you good news! Christ has redeemed us from the curse of our sinful mistakes by suffering the curse for us.

Galatians 3:13
"Christ redeemed us from the curse of the law by becoming a curse for us, for it is written: 'Cursed is everyone who is hung on a tree.'"

Lord Jesus, deliver me from the curse of my sins and the unintended consequences. Set me free that I may serve You. In Your holy name I pray. Amen.

ONE MINUTE
DEVOTIONS

APRIL 20

As I look back over my life, I realize that I have missed a number of opportunities—opportunities to be forgiving, to speak a word of apology, to lend a helping hand, or to offer the gift of friendship. Some opportunities are gone forever. Others linger still, giving me another chance. With God's help, I will not let a single expression of love go unspoken; I won't leave a single act of kindness undone, a single friendship unpursued. I dare not, for life is too fleeting and I may never get another chance. You may not either, so seize the moment!

Proverbs 3:27
"Do not withhold good from those who deserve it, when it is in your power to act."

Lord Jesus, help me to seize the moment and live life in the Spirit to the fullest. In Your holy name I pray. Amen.

ONE MINUTE
DEVOTIONS

APRIL 21

Most of us can overcome any adversity if we can be assured of three things. First, we must know that God cares. Then, we must be convinced that He won't forsake us. Finally, we have to know that God will redeem our situation. As rational creatures, the thought that a tragic life-altering event might be pointless is simply unbearable. But if we know that God will ultimately bring good out of what looks like a senseless tragedy, we can somehow bear it.

2 Corinthians 1:9-10
"But this happened that we might not rely on ourselves but on God, who raises the dead. He has delivered us from such a deadly peril, and he will deliver us. On him we have set our hope."

Lord Jesus, no matter what life throws at me, You are my hope and my deliverer. Teach me to trust You more. In Your holy name I pray. Amen.

ONE MINUTE
DEVOTIONS

APRIL 22

When you look around what do you see—shattered dreams, a failed business, family problems, an impending divorce? That's all there. No one can deny it, but if that's all you see, you're only seeing with one eye. If you open both eyes, you will not only see what is—the tragedies of life—but also what can be. If you look with the eye of faith, you will see joy and possibilities where you were sure none existed. You might even see a miracle in the making, for with God nothing is impossible (Luke 1:37).

Luke 18:27
"What is impossible with men is possible with God."

Lord Jesus, open my eyes so I can see not only what is, but also what can be. In Your holy name I pray. Amen.

ONE
MINUTE
DEVOTIONS

APRIL 23

When you're in Gethsemane, the situation can look hopeless. No matter how desperately you pray, things never seem to get any better. Worst of all, it feels like God has forsaken you. The sense of His nearness that once sustained you seems to have vanished. It feels like you have been left to wander alone in the darkness, stumbling over the wreckage of your world. But you are only seeing with one eye, the natural eye. For those who refuse to give up, who dare to see with both eyes—the natural eye and the spiritual eye—there's something beyond the darkness, something beyond the pain and brokenness of our shattered world.

Romans 8:18
"Our present sufferings are not worth comparing with the glory that will be revealed in us."

Lord Jesus, help me to look beyond my present circumstances to my eternal destiny. In Your holy name I pray. Amen.

ONE MINUTE
DEVOTIONS

APRIL 24

Once, I asked an astute businessman the secret of his success. With a slow smile, he raised his finger and pointed toward the ceiling. When I pressed him for something more definitive than divine help he said, "Never fall in love with the deal. A deal is like a beautiful woman. Once you fall in love with her, you lose all objectivity. Passion takes over, distorting your judgment. You maximize the upside while minimizing the downside. In short, you turn a blind eye to the risks."

Proverbs 28:19
"The one who chases fantasies will have his fill of poverty."

Lord Jesus, protect me from my fantasies and help me to never fall in love with the deal. In Your holy name Ipray. Amen.

ONE MINUTE DEVOTIONS

APRIL 25

Change often requires us to face new challenges and learn new skills with the accompanying risks. The church must change the way it functions to meet the varied and complex demands of people living in the twenty-first century. If we try to hang onto the old ways of doing ministry, we will be left behind, yet that's exactly what we're tempted to do. Are there risks inherent in change? Absolutely, but the risks of trying to recreate the past are even greater.

Genesis 19:26
"But Lot's wife looked back, and she became a pillar of salt."

Lord Jesus, I can't live in the past or I will die, but if we forget the past, I will lose my way. Help me to appreciate the past without trying to recreate it and to embrace the future with faith. In Your holy name I pray. Amen.

ONE MINUTE DEVOTIONS

APRIL 26

Is your life on hold? Have you been looking back instead of casting vision for the future? Is fear holding you back—fear of failure or even just fear of the unknown? If my experience is any indication, fear, or at least uncertainty, is usually part of any undertaking, but we don't have to let it paralyze us. Fear can imprison us or we can use it to motivate us. The choice is ours!

2 Corinthians 7:5
"For when we came into Macedonia, this body of ours had no rest, but we were harassed at every turn – conflicts on the outside, fears within."

Lord Jesus, even though I experience fear, don't let it determine my destiny. Give me the courage to overcome my fears because I trust in You. In Your holy name I pray. Amen.

ONE MINUTE

DEVOTIONS

APRIL 27

Are you walking through a difficult time right now? Are you dealing with disappointment or coping with loss? Perhaps you feel overwhelmed, as if the Lord has forsaken you. I've been there and I know how it feels. I won't lie to you. There have been times when the pain was nearly more than I could bear, but always God sustained me. He is no respecter of persons and what He has done for me He will do for you.

2 Corinthians 1:8-9
"We were under great pressure, far beyond our ability to endure…this happened that we might not rely on ourselves but on God."

Lord Jesus, when life overwhelms me teach me to rely on You. In Your holy name I pray. Amen.

ONE MINUTE
DEVOTIONS

APRIL 28

A re you walking through a dark place in your life? Does it seem God has forsaken you? Are you tempted to give up? Don't! Instead choose to trust God, even though disappointment and loss may have made it impossible for you to understand His ways. Like an unerring compass, His Word will guide you safely through the fog of your pain. No matter how great your disappointment, God can turn your heartbreak into hope. Your past does not have to determine your destiny.

Jeremiah 29:11
"For I know the plans I have for you...plans to prosper you and not to harm you, plans to give you hope and a future."

Lord Jesus, I choose to trust You no matter how dark the night. Help me to trust You more. In Your holy name I pray. Amen.

ONE MINUTE DEVOTIONS

APRIL 29

Trust God in your darkest hour. Trust Him even when it seems to make no sense and all the evidence seems to say He has let you down. Trust Him when the heavens turn to brass and your most desperate prayers seem to go unanswered. Trust Him no matter what and He will grant you a supernatural peace that is not dependent on circumstances or understanding.

Philippians 4:7
"The peace of God, which transcends all understanding, will guard your hearts and your minds in Christ Jesus."

Lord Jesus, I choose to trust You no matter what is happening in my life. Grant me Your supernatural peace. In Your holy name I pray. Amen.

ONE MINUTE
DEVOTIONS

APRIL 30

When asked, "What does love look like?" St. Augustine replied, "It has hands to help others. It has feet to hasten to the poor and needy. It has eyes to see misery and want. It has ears to hear the sighs and sorrow of men. That is what love looks like." I call that 'blue-collar Christianity,' the Gospel in shoe leather, love with its sleeves rolled up, caring enough to get involved.

1 John 3:16,18
"We ought to lay down our lives for our brothers...let us not love with words...but with actions and in truth."

Lord Jesus, help me to roll up my sleeves and wade into life's messiness, dispensing love no matter the risk. In Your holy name I pray. Amen.

ONE MINUTE
DEVOTIONS

MAY 1

What does true Christian love look like? It's caring enough to get involved. It takes a chance on getting hurt or being let down, knowing that taking the risk is better than playing it safe and maybe never knowing either the pain or joy of really loving. Unfortunately, it's a lot easier to limit our Christian service to safe things that let us feel like we're serving without running the risk of getting our hands dirty.

Acts 20:24
"I consider my life worth nothing to me, if only I may finish the race and complete the task the Lord Jesus has given me."

Lord Jesus, teach my to get my hands dirty caring for others. When I get hurt in love's service, bind up my wounds and send me back into this messiness called life. In Your holy name I pray. Amen.

ONE MINUTE
DEVOTIONS

MAY 2

I had just returned from a long trip. I was tired, wanting to rest. The telephone rang. It was Hector. Would I meet him for coffee? I knew he needed a friend so I went, but I didn't want to. There in a secluded booth sat a lonely man, feeling little worth, bruised and hurt by life. I gave him the gift of my presence in Jesus' name and slowly he began to hope again, to feel like his life might have meaning. I returned home exhausted in body, but exhilarated in my spirit.

Galatians 6:2
"Carry each other's burdens, and in this way you will fulfill the law of Christ."

Lord Jesus, help me lay down my life in loving service for others. In Your holy name I pray. Amen.

ONE MINUTE DEVOTIONS

MAY 3

Do you want a ministry? Look around you. What do you see? Probably needy people within arm's reach—a spouse you've been too busy to love, a teenager you've never taken time to understand, a child who hardly knows you. Or maybe it's the person you work with. The one you've written off as antisocial, the troublemaker. Do you have any idea why she's so angry, so defensive? You can start by loving that person. That can be your ministry!

Galatians 6:9
"Let us not become weary in doing good, for at the proper time we will reap a harvest if we do not give up."

Lord Jesus, help me to love those who are not easy to love. In Your holy name I pray. Amen.

ONE MINUTE DEVOTIONS

MAY 4

Have you ever gotten ahead of God? That's called misguided zeal and it always tempts us to do things God has not called us to do. These are usually not bad things, in fact they are often "good" things but they are not "God" things. The key to resisting this temptation is to have a clear understanding of your call and an uncompromising commitment to the One who called you.

2 Timothy 4:7-8
"I have fought the good fight, I have finished the race, I have kept the faith. Now there is in store for me the crown of righteousness, which the Lord, the righteous Judge, will award to me on that day."

Lord Jesus, may I always be obedient rather than ambitious and ever faithful to Your call. In Your holy name I pray. Amen.

ONE MINUTE DEVOTIONS

MAY 5

May you always have the courage to be obedient to the One who called you, no matter what the cost. Yet in your faithful obedience may you be humble not proud, gentle not overbearing, and loving not manipulative. May others see the Spirit of Christ in you and be drawn to Him. May the fragrance of His presence permeate every encounter you have.

Acts 4:13
"When they saw the courage of Peter and John and realized that they were unschooled, ordinary men, they were astonished and they took note that these men had been with Jesus."

Lord Jesus, fill me with Your holy presence that the power of Your life may permeate all of my relationships. In Your holy name I pray. Amen.

ONE MINUTE DEVOTIONS

MAY 6

Fasting is hard for me. Not only do I crave food, but I also hunger for the fellowship of mealtime—the camaraderie, the conversation. That's one of the reasons we are called to fast—so we can learn to satisfy our deepest belonging needs in relationship with the Lord. In truth, meaning and fulfillment are found only in relationship with Him.

Psalm 42:1-2
"As the deer pants for streams of water, so my soul pants for you, O God. My soul thirsts for God, for the living God."

Lord Jesus, give me the strength to fast, the strength to satisfy my deepest belonging needs in relationship with You and You alone. In Your holy name I pray. Amen.

ONE MINUTE
DEVOTIONS

MAY 7

Life is hectic and our best intentions frequently fall prey to a relentless busyness. Sadly, one of the first things to go for many of us is our devotional life. As a result, we feel like a spiritual failure. We love the Lord so we vow to do better, but our guilt lingers and like a low-grade fever, it drains our life of its vitality. Maybe the answer is to live conscious of God each moment, no matter how busy we are.

Psalm 119:37
"Turn my eyes away from worthless things; preserve my life according to your word."

Lord Jesus, let my first thought each morning be of You and my last thought each night. May I be ever conscious of Your presence. In Your holy name I pray. Amen.

ONE MINUTE DEVOTIONS

MAY 8

God invites us to bring our heartfelt emotions to Him, even the ones we think we shouldn't have. As we pour out our deepest feelings in honest confession and sincere prayer, He helps us move from hurt and confusion to acceptance, and finally, to unconditional trust. The only things beyond the reach of God's healing grace are those things we refuse to acknowledge and bring to Him.

Psalm 33:18; 32:10
"The eyes of the LORD are on those who fear him, on those whose hope is in his unfailing love...the LORD's unfailing love surrounds the man who trusts in him."

Lord Jesus, help me to trust Your unfailing love and to pour out my heart to You without holding anything back. In Your holy name I pray. Amen.

ONE MINUTE DEVOTIONS

MAY 9

God has given every believer the gift of abundant life—that is, the potential for abundant life—but it is up to us to exercise the spiritual disciplines that will make it a reality in our life. For me, that means practicing the rhythm of life—that delicate balance between work, rest, worship, and play. Let me ignore the rhythm God has woven into the very fabric of creation and my life soon loses its spiritual and emotional vitality.

Isaiah 40:31
"Those who hope in the Lord will renew their strength. They will soar on wings like eagles; they will run and not grow weary, they will walk and not be faint."

Lord Jesus, deliver me from my frantic busyness and teach me to live in rhythm with You. In Your holy name I pray. Amen.

ONE MINUTE DEVOTIONS

MAY 10

God is not only a heavenly Father who cares about us, but also One who has the power to intervene on our behalf. When life comes crashing down around us it is good to know that God cares, but we need more than that. We need to know that God is greater than any storm we face and that He can turn our situation around!

Isaiah 41:10
"Do not fear, for I am with you; do not be dismayed, for I am your God. I will strengthen you and help you; I will uphold you with my righteous right hand."

Heavenly Father, I thank You for Your great compassion and Your unfailing love. I am especially thankful that with You, all things are possible. In Your holy name I pray. Amen.

ONE MINUTE DEVOTIONS

MAY 11

To be effective in life and ministry, we need both vision and relationships. Vision expands our horizons and energizes us, while relationships nurture us and keep us grounded. Vision without relationships exposes us to unholy ambition. Relationships without vision tempt us to become self-centered and narcissistic. But when vision and relationship marry, there is nothing that cannot be accomplished for God.

Mark 3:14-15
"He appointed twelve – designating them apostles – that they might be with him and that he might send them out to preach and to have authority to drive out demons."

Lord Jesus, teach me to spend time with You so that You can send me out to minister for You. In Your holy name I pray. Amen.

ONE MINUTE DEVOTIONS

MAY 12

If you really want to know what a person is like, put them under pressure. As heat and light emanate from fire, so is a person's character revealed when things get tough. In the crucible of interpersonal relationships, the nature of our heart is made known. In moments of pressure or confrontation, our true self is revealed.

Matthew 12:34-35
"For out of the overflow of the heart the mouth speaks. The good man brings good things out of the good stored up in him, and the evil man brings evil things out of the evil stored up in him."

Lord Jesus, make me a person of character. Create in me a heart filled with compassion and integrity. In Your holy name I pray. Amen.

ONE MINUTE
DEVOTIONS

MAY 13

To truly worship God, to draw near to Him with our whole heart, means to bare our souls before Him, holding nothing back—not the good, the bad, or the ugly. The reality of who He is and how He loves us is so totally disarming that we come into His presence without fear or pretense, but not without reverence, which is to say that we are fully ourselves, totally transparent, and wonderfully alive.

Isaiah 6:6-7
"Then one of the seraphs flew to me with a live coal in his hand...With it he touched my mouth and said, '... your guilt is taken away and your sin atoned for.'"

Lord Jesus, thank You for Your unconditional love that welcomes me into Your presence and for Your holy fire that cleanses and makes me new. In Your holy name I pray. Amen.

ONE MINUTE DEVOTIONS

MAY 14

Loving service, humble service, in a place where no-body sees and nobody knows, is what transforms personal power into redemptive ministry. Only in serving others are we saved from our selfish selves and from the perils of power.

Philippians 2:3-5

"Do nothing out of selfish ambition or vain conceit, but in humility consider others better than yourselves. Each of you should look not only to your own interests, but also to the interests of others. Your attitude should be the same as that of Christ Jesus."

Lord Jesus, help me to lay aside the trappings of power and take up a basin of water and a towel and go forth in loving service. In Your holy name me pray. Amen.

ONE MINUTE DEVOTIONS

MAY 15

I don't want to admit it, but I am my own worst enemy. Most of us are. Left to our own desires we will destroy ourselves. We will sacrifice those we love on the altar of ambition. Pride will lead us astray, causing us to compromise our integrity in a misguided attempt to prove ourselves. Well it has been said, "We have met the enemy and he is us."

Matthew 16:25
"For whoever wants to save his life will lose it, but whoever loses his life for me will find it."

Lord Jesus, teach me to be obedient rather than ambitious. Help me to seek to please only You; not my selfish self or even others, simply You. In Your holy name I pray. Amen.

ONE MINUTE DEVOTIONS

MAY 16

The sacrifice of praise may not alter our painful circumstances, but it does put them into eternal perspective. Seen through the lens of loss or disappointment, God seems small and far away—it's like looking at Him through the wrong end of a telescope. Praise reverses the telescope. Now God is very near and greater than all our troubles.

Psalm 86:6-7
"Hear my prayer, O Lord; listen to my cry for mercy. In the day of my trouble I will call to you, for you will answer me."

Lord Jesus, teach me to remember all You have done for me and to pray God-centered prayers rather than need-centered prayers. In Your holy name I pray. Amen.

ONE MINUTE
DEVOTIONS

MAY 17

As you discipline yourself to wait quietly in the Lord's presence, you will feel the tensions slip away. Even the discordant voices within will grow quiet. Out of the silence God will speak to you in a still small voice that renews your soul. You will remember who you are—a child of God. You will remember who He is—your Heavenly Father. You will remember and be blessed.

Isaiah 26:3 KJV
"Thou wilt keep him in perfect peace, whose mind is stayed on thee: because he trusteth in thee."

Lord Jesus, it is hard for me to be still, to wait quietly in Your presence. A half a hundred thoughts clamor for my attention and the demands of the day press in upon me. Still I wait, for only Your still small voice can renew me. In Your holy name I pray. Amen.

ONE MINUTE DEVOTIONS

MAY 18

Are you having difficulty hearing God's voice? Perhaps you're trying too hard. Relax. Be still. Hearing God's voice grows out of relationship with Him. Sometimes He speaks as we linger in His presence. At other times He speaks to us in the stress and busyness of our lives. And sometimes He speaks to us out of the storm. But of this one thing you may be sure, God wants you to hear His voice even more than you want to hear it and He will make His will known to you.

John 10:4
"When he has brought out all his own, he goes on ahead of them, and his sheep follow him because they know his voice."

Lord Jesus, there are many voices clamoring for my attention, but it is Your voice I long to hear. Help me to recognize it, in spite of all the distractions. In Your holy name I pray. Amen.

ONE MINUTE DEVOTIONS

MAY 19

Nothing can change the past. Not even God. But with God's help you can change how you look at the past and even how you feel about it. What happened in the past isn't what is destroying you; it's what you're doing to yourself because of the past. Stop punishing yourself. Stop blaming others, or even God. Embrace the future with faith and you will be amazed at what God will do.

Philippians 3:13-14
"One thing I do: Forgetting what is behind and straining toward what is ahead, I press on toward the goal to win the prize for which God has called me heavenward in Christ Jesus."

Lord Jesus, help me to forget the past with its hurts and disappointments. Don't let them imprison me. Set me free to become all You have called me to be. In Your holy name I pray. Amen.

ONE MINUTE DEVOTIONS

MAY 20

Are you constantly reliving the painful experiences in your past, trying to understand why those things happened to you? The truth you seek won't be found in the past. Knowing "how" or "what" or "why" won't change anything. There's only one thing that will heal your troubled heart—not answers or even understanding, but only unconditional trust in the wisdom and sovereignty of God.

Job 13:15-16
"Though he slay me, yet will I hope in him…Indeed, this will turn out for my deliverance."

Lord Jesus, help me to stop fixating on the past, to stop trying to figure it out. Even if I could, it wouldn't change a thing. Instead give me the grace to trust You with both my past and my future. In Your holy name I pray. Amen.

ONE MINUTE DEVOTIONS

MAY 21

To make wise decisions we must know our core values—the values that shape our lives. For instance, my core values are: 1) Absolute obedience to Jesus Christ; 2) A commitment to empowering others to be all God has called them to be; and 3) A commitment to excellence in everything I do. Every decision you make should honor your core values. Any decision that compromises them creates internal conflict and undermines your effectiveness.

2 Timothy 1:14
"Guard the good deposit that was entrusted to you – guard it with the help of the Holy Spirit who lives in us."

Lord Jesus, help my to be true to the eternal values You have given me. May I always make wise decisions that fulfill Your purposes. In Your holy name I pray. Amen.

ONE MINUTE DEVOTIONS

MAY 22

Worry tempts us to try and solve problems that have not yet happened and may never happen. When we worry, we are on our own because God does not give us wisdom for imaginary problems or grace for imaginary trials. So what can we do? "Do not be anxious about anything, but in everything, by prayer and petition, with thanksgiving, present your requests to God. And the peace of God, which transcends all understanding, will guard your hearts and your minds in Christ Jesus" (Philippians 4:6-7).

1 Peter 5:6-7
"Humble yourselves, therefore, under God's mighty hand, that he may lift you up in due time. Cast all your anxiety on him because he cares for you."

Lord Jesus, when I am tempted to worry, help me to pray. Help me to focus on Your sufficiency, not my imaginary problems. In Your holy name I pray. Amen.

ONE MINUTE
DEVOTIONS

MAY 23

You can't live very long without realizing that no one is immune to the storms of life, not even believers, no matter how strong their faith. The real difference then, between the believer and the unbeliever, is not that one is spared from life's inevitable storms while the other is not, but that in Christ the believer has resources to overcome the storm, regardless of how severe it may be.

Acts 27:22,25
"But now I urge you to keep up your courage, because not one of you will be lost...I have faith in God that it will happen just as he told me."

Lord Jesus, teach me to trust You no matter how violent the storm. Give me Your peace. In Your holy name I pray. Amen.

ONE MINUTE DEVOTIONS

MAY 24

When we are tempted, God is not only faithful to provide a way of escape, but He often uses the very temptation the enemy intended for our destruction to produce spiritual maturity in us. I best understand how God does this when I compare it to the way an expert in self-defense uses his opponent's weight and momentum against him. In the same way, God turns the enemy's attack to our advantage.

James 1:2-4 NKJV
"Count it all joy when you fall into various trials, knowing that the testing of your faith produces patience... that you may be perfect and complete, lacking nothing."

Lord Jesus, thank You for redeeming every situation I face, for turning each one to my eternal advantage. In Your holy name I pray. Amen.

ONE
MINUTE
DEVOTIONS

MAY 25

If you are suffering from a chronic illness, you may be wondering what you can do to receive your healing. First, fill your mind with the miracles of Jesus. Think on them. By faith, see yourself healed. Second, get rid of all hurt and bitterness. Nothing poisons our spirit faster than unforgiveness. Finally, step out in faith. Get out of your comfort zone. Attend a meeting where they pray for the sick and ask for prayer.

Acts 3:16
"It is Jesus' name and the faith that comes through him that has given this complete healing."

Lord Jesus, I believe all things are possible, even the healing of incurable diseases. Help me to believe more. Intervene on my behalf. In Your holy name I pray. Amen.

ONE MINUTE DEVOTIONS

MAY 26

While Jesus lived on this earth, He was both the Son of God and the Son of Man. In His public ministry we see the Christ—the glory of the One who came from the Father, full of grace and truth. In the private moments He spent with the disciples, we see Jesus, Mary's son. The One who was made like us in every way (see Hebrews 2:17). We worship the glorified Son of God, but we love Jesus, the One who shared our humanity.

Hebrews 4:15-16
"For we do not have a high priest who is unable to empathize with our weaknesses, but we have one who has been tempted in every way, just as we are—yet he did not sin. Let us then approach God's throne of grace with confidence, so that we may receive mercy and find grace to help us in our time of need."

Lord Jesus, thank You for becoming the Son of Man that I might be made the son of God. In Your holy name I pray. Amen.

ONE MINUTE
DEVOTIONS

MAY 27

Jesus was both the Son of God and the Son of Man. As a man, He became physically exhausted. Once He was so tired that He slept through a life-threatening storm, yet as the divine Son of God, He commanded the storm to cease. As a man, He was so deeply grieved by the death of His friend Lazarus that He wept. As the Son of God, He raised Lazarus from the dead! As the Son of Man, he empathizes with us; as the Son of God, He intervenes on our behalf.

John 1:14
"The Word became flesh and made his dwelling among us. We have seen his glory, the glory of the one and only Son, who came from the Father, full of grace and truth."

Lord Jesus, You shared my humanity, therefore I approach You with confidence. You not only know what I am feeling, but you care about me and you can also deliver me. Help me, I pray, in Your holy name. Amen.

ONE MINUTE DEVOTIONS

MAY 28

The Holy Spirit is always very specific when He convicts us of sin. He puts His finger on it, identifies it so we can bring it to God and get rid of it. Condemnation is vague, general; it leaves us feeling guilty, unworthy, but not really sure why. It does not identify a particular sin, lest we deal with it and be delivered. In fact, the only time condemnation is specific is when it condemns us of sins we've already confessed.

2 Corinthians 7:10 (explanation mine)
"Godly sorrow [conviction] brings repentance that leads to salvation and leaves no regret, but worldly sorrow [condemnation] brings death."

Lord Jesus, help me to discern between the conviction of the Holy Spirit and the condemnation of the enemy that I may walk in victory. In Your holy name I pray. Amen.

ONE MINUTE DEVOTIONS

MAY 29

Holy Spirit conviction makes us painfully aware of our sinfulness, yet even as it does, we are motivated to confess our sins and try again. It draws us to God. Condemnation, on the other hand, makes us feel like giving up. It tells us that we will never be any different, that God is sick of our repeated failures and ready to wash His hands of us. It drives us into hiding, away from God.

Romans 8:1 KJV
"There is therefore now no condemnation to them which are in Christ Jesus, who walk not after the flesh, but after the Spirit."

Lord Jesus, I confess my sins and receive Your forgiveness. Now let me walk in holy freedom, free from all condemnation. In Your holy name I pray. Amen.

ONE MINUTE
DEVOTIONS

MAY 30

Character and competence are two sides of the same coin. Character focuses on who we are. Competence focuses on what we do. Character is about being—being God's person in every situation. Competence is about doing God's work in every situation. Character is what God is doing in us—i.e. conforming us to the likeness of his Son (Romans 8:29). Competence is about what God is doing through us—i.e. acts of Christian service.

Exodus 18:21
"But select capable men from all the people – men who fear God, trustworthy men who hate dishonest gain – and appoint them as officials over thousands, hundreds, fifties, and tens."

Lord Jesus, develop my character as I spend time being with You. Develop my competency as I am doing ministry. In Your holy name I pray. Amen.

ONE
MINUTE
DEVOTIONS

MAY 31

When I think of a man of character my thoughts always turn to my Uncle Ernie. He was not a great man as the world counts greatness. He was, however, a special man, a throwback to an earlier age when the measure of a man was determined by the quality of his character rather than the power of his personality. In truth, he was one of those men who "wore well"—that is, the longer you knew him the more you appreciated him.

1 Timothy 3:2,7
"Now the overseer must be above reproach…He must also have a good reputation with outsiders."

Lord Jesus, help me to be a person of character, that Your name may be praised. In Your holy name I pray. Amen.

ONE MINUTE DEVOTIONS

JUNE 1

To be a person of character is not complicated. You live modestly, love your neighbor as yourself, turn the other cheek, forgive others as Christ has forgiven you, keep your word, pay your debts on time, and honor your commitments. You provide for your family, honor your marriage vows, love your spouse, train your children in the nurture and admonition of the Lord, and honor the Lord in all you do and say.

1 Timothy 4:15,16
"Be diligent in these matters… Watch your life and doctrine closely."

Lord Jesus, help me to be diligent and conscientious in my daily life, always reflecting Your holy love. In Your name I pray. Amen.

ONE MINUTE
DEVOTIONS

JUNE 2

One of the keys to success is to recognize your strengths—that is your God-given abilities—and build on them. Many of us are tempted to focus on our weaknesses in order to improve in those areas where we are less gifted. As a result, we fail to maximize our areas of giftedness and limit our effectiveness. We also experience a diminishing return. Instead of renewing us, our work exhausts us.

Exodus 18:17-18

"'What you are doing is not good. You and these people who come to you will only wear yourselves out.'"

Lord Jesus, help me to focus on my strengths and not my weaknesses, that I may accomplish all You have called me to do. In Your holy name I pray. Amen.

ONE MINUTE
DEVOTIONS

JUNE 3

No one can do everything and the sooner we realize this, the better off everyone will be. It is not weakness but wisdom that prompts the leader to surround himself with a highly effective team. To be a competent leader does not mean you have to master the multiplicity of tasks required to lead a highly successful organization, but only that you are wise enough to build a team that is able to effectively manage those tasks.

Acts 6:2-4
"So the Twelve gathered all the disciples together and said, 'It would not be right for us to neglect the ministry of the word of God in order to wait on tables. Brothers and sisters, choose seven men from among you who are known to be full of the Spirit and wisdom. We will turn this responsibility over to them and will give our attention to prayer and the ministry of the word."

Lord Jesus, give me the self-confidence and the wisdom to build an effective team. In Your holy name I pray. Amen.

ONE MINUTE
DEVOTIONS

JUNE 4

The devotional life is multidimensional, but the three most critical disciplines are prayer, study, and fasting. What breath is to the body, prayer is to the soul. It restores our spiritual vitality. It shapes us into God's image. It brings our thoughts and feelings into perfect accord with the Father's desires. It enlarges our vision and enables us to think God's thoughts after Him. It puts all of life into perspective and brings eternity into focus.

Luke 9:28-29
"Jesus...went up onto a mountain to pray. As he was praying, the appearance of his face changed."

Lord Jesus, teach me to pray the kinds of prayers that transform me. Change not only my appearance, but also my character. In Your holy name I pray. Amen.

ONE
MINUTE
DEVOTIONS

JUNE 5

To the subjective discipline of prayer we add the objective discipline of study, especially the study of God's Word. Even as we study the Word, we remind ourselves that it is bread to be eaten, not literature to be admired. We are continually putting it into practice and letting it change our life. For our devotional life to be complete we need to read devotional classics and other books that deal with the inner life. It is enormously beneficial to learn from the experience of those who have walked this way before us.

2 Timothy 2:15 KJV
"Study to shew thyself approved unto God, a workman that needeth not to be ashamed, rightly dividing the word of truth."

Lord Jesus, help me to hide Your Word in my heart that I might be transformed until I am conformed to Your likeness. In Your holy name I pray. Amen.

ONE
MINUTE
DEVOTIONS

JUNE 6

A lthough believers do not normally give fasting the same attention they give prayer and Bible reading, the Scriptures put it in the same category. Arthur Wallis writes in *God's Chosen Fast*, "Neither did Jesus say, if you, as though fasting were something the disciples might or might not be led to do...He stated unambiguously and without qualification, 'When you fast...' He left us in no doubt that He took it for granted that His disciples would be obeying the leading of the Spirit in this matter of fasting."

Matthew 6:17-18
"When you fast...your Father, who sees what is done is secret, will reward you."

Lord Jesus, give me the discipline to fast regularly as part of my devotional life. In Your holy name I pray. Amen.

ONE
MINUTE
DEVOTIONS

JUNE 7

In prayer, Jesus experienced fellowship with the Father that nourished His soul. He received guidance to direct Him in His life's work and anointing to accomplish His ministry. It was the single most important discipline of His earthly existence and the source of His strength. If prayer was critical to the life and ministry of our Lord—and obviously it was—how much more critical is it for those of us who would be Christ- followers today?

Luke 18:1
"Then Jesus told his disciples a parable to show them that they should always pray and not give up."

Lord Jesus, forgive me when I get too busy to pray. Slow me down and call me into a quiet place where I can fellowship with You. In Your holy name I pray. Amen.

ONE MINUTE DEVOTIONS

JUNE 8

Devotional praying helps us become the people God has called us to be. It focuses on matters of the heart and causes us to examine ourselves and our relationships in light of God's Holy Word. We are not talking about morbid introspection but the sanctifying work of the Holy Spirit. Early in our walk with the Lord, our temptations are generally the more obvious temptations of the flesh—lust, ambition, and materialism. But as we grow in the Lord, they become the more subtle temptations of the heart. These are temptations that only the Word and the Spirit can root out.

Psalm 139:23-24
"Search me, O God, and know my heart…See if there is any offensive way in me."

Lord Jesus, help me to take responsibility for my attitudes so I can be changed by Your Holy Spirit. In Your holy name I pray. Amen.

ONE MINUTE DEVOTIONS

JUNE 9

Journaling has been an important part of my devotional praying for years. It is a historical spiritual discipline and the keeping of prayer journals has played a significant role in the history of the Church. From St. Augustine to Pascal to the Society of Friends, some form of the spiritual journal has been used for spiritual discipline and growth. It is a wise person who learns from those who have gone before him and puts this ancient discipline into practice in his own life.

Proverbs 20:27
"The lamp of the LORD searches the spirit of a man, it searches out his inmost being."

Lord Jesus, guide my thoughts as I reflect upon my daily walk. Reveal things I would not ordinarily see. In Your holy name I pray. Amen.

ONE MINUTE DEVOTIONS

JUNE 10

As a young man I considered prayer an obligation, something Christians had to do. As I matured in the Lord, I came to understand that it was a discipline that would one day become a delight. Now I realize that prayer is a privilege. Try to get an audience with some earthly dignitary and what do you think your chances are? Probably not every good, but every time we whisper a prayer in Jesus' name, God promises to meet us there. Now that's a privilege!

2 Chronicles 7:14
"If my people, who are called by my name, will humble themselves and pray and seek my face and turn from their wicked ways, then I will hear from heaven, and I will forgive their sin and will heal their land."

Lord Jesus, thank You for always being there when I call upon You. In Your holy name I pray. Amen.

ONE MINUTE
DEVOTIONS

JUNE 11

When we read the Bible devotionally, we do so in order to answer three questions. First, "What is the historical setting?" The second question is, "What does this passage say about God?" The third question is more personal: "What does this passage say to me about my spiritual condition, about my life, and my standing with God?" When we read the Scriptures, we need to act on what we are learning. As Richard Foster says, "When we come to the Scripture we come to be changed, not to amass information."

Psalm 119:11 NKJV
"Your word I have hidden in my heart, that I might not sin against You."

Lord Jesus, use the Word to shape me, to conform me to Your very own image. In Your holy name I pray. Amen.

ONE MINUTE
DEVOTIONS

JUNE 12

I am told that in the Library of Congress there is a copy of the United States Constitution, which, when viewed from a certain angle, seems to bear a portrait of George Washington, the father of our country. So it is with the Scriptures. When we read them with faith they are more than just a collection of ancient poetry or proverbs, they are a revelation of God himself, a portrait of our heavenly Father.

Ephesians 1:17
"I keep asking that the God of our Lord Jesus Christ, the glorious Father, may give you the Spirit of wisdom and revelation so that you may know him better."

Lord Jesus, open my eyes and my understanding as I read the Scriptures. Let me come to know You in ever increasing ways. In Your holy name I pray. Amen.

ONE MINUTE DEVOTIONS

JUNE 13

Several years ago, I was going through a difficult period. One morning during my devotional time, I was reading in the Psalms when I came across Psalm 138. Although I had read that passage numerous times before, that particular morning the words seemed to leap off the page. "Though I walk in the midst of trouble…The Lord will fulfill his purpose for me…." Although my situation did not immediately change, I was at peace. God had spoken to me through His Word. No matter what others did, He would fulfill His purpose in my life. And He will do the same for you.

Psalm 139:16
"All the days ordained for me, were written in your book before one of them came to be."

Lord Jesus, fulfill Your purposes in my life. In Your holy name I pray. Amen.

ONE MINUTE DEVOTIONS

JUNE 14

I do not limit my devotional reading to the Scriptures, nor should you. Of course the Scriptures are the only infallible Word and everything else we read must be weighed against them. Still, having said that, let me hasten to add that reading a book written by an author whose heart and mind is steeped in God's eternal truth is like sitting at the feet of a truly wise man. His writings are a fountain of life.

Proverbs 13:14
"The teaching of the wise is a fountain of life, turning a man from the snares of death."

Lord Jesus, thank You for those gifted men and women whose writings and teachings instruct me in the way of life. Bless and keep them. In Your holy name I pray.

ONE MINUTE
DEVOTIONS

JUNE 15

If you are not a reader, you are depriving yourself of one of God's best gifts. A good book renews us in a way nothing else can. I'm not necessarily talking about weighty books that tax the mind, but insightful books that touch the soul—books that give us a glimpse of life in both its tenderness and its tragedy. Books that put us in touch with God and our own life experiences. As far as I am concerned, any book that can do that is worth whatever it costs and more.

Ecclesiastes 3:11
"(God) has made everything beautiful in its time. He has also set eternity in the hearts of men."

Lord Jesus, thank You for the many books that have enriched my soul and enlightened my mind. Bless those men and women who have poured out their souls to prepare food for my soul. In Your holy name I pray. Amen.

ONE MINUTE
DEVOTIONS

JUNE 16

The books that appeal to you will likely vary depending on the season of life in which you find yourself. On more than one occasion, I have started reading a highly recommended book only to lay it aside in frustration after a chapter or two. Was the book overrated or poorly written? Maybe, but more likely I was not spiritually or emotionally ready for it. Sometimes I will return to the same book a year or two later and find that I cannot put it down. I am in a different season of life and it now speaks to my soul.

Proverbs 3:13
"Blessed is the man who finds wisdom."

Lord Jesus, thank You for the wisdom hidden in the pages of books. Speak to me, not only by Your Spirit, but also through the writings of godly men and women. In Your holy name I pray. Amen.

ONE
MINUTE
DEVOTIONS

JUNE 17

Only God knows how many books He has used to touch me, change me, and make me more the person He has called me to be. Some of the more memorable ones are, *A Touch of Wonder* by Arthur Gordon, *Tuesdays with Morrie* by Mitch Albom, and *Windows of the Soul* by Ken Gire. The authors that speak to you may not be the same ones that speak to me, and that's okay. The important thing is to find books that nourish your soul and put you in touch with life and God.

Proverbs 7:2
"Guard my teachings as the apple of your eye."

Lord Jesus, bless the writers who bring Your truth to all of us. In Your holy name I pray. Amen.

ONE MINUTE
DEVOTIONS

JUNE 18

The account of Mary and Martha teaches us that nothing is more important than our relationship with the Lord. The work that Martha was doing was important but not as important as being with Jesus. Mary sat at His feet listening to Him and Jesus concluded, "Mary has chosen what is better" (Luke 10:42). It is the Lord's way of telling us that "being" is more important than "doing" and that relationship always comes before ministry.

Luke 10:41-42
"'Martha, Martha,' the Lord answered, 'you are worried and upset about many things, but few things are needed – or indeed only one. Mary has chosen what is better, and it will not be taken away from her.'"

Lord Jesus, help me to always focus on my relationship with You without ignoring my work for You. In Your holy name I pray. Amen.

ONE MINUTE
DEVOTIONS

JUNE 19

Do you struggle with a besetting sin? Don't despair, God is greater than any stronghold in your life. For years I was an angry man. I used a number of strategies in an attempt to control my anger. I suffered in silence and grew bitter. I lashed out in retaliation and lived to regret it. I tried to give in and ended up feeling used and trapped. I confronted in love, tough love, and grieved as I was misunderstood and feared. Here's what I discovered. Anger management techniques are largely ineffective until the stronghold of anger is broken. Only God can break that stronghold, but you must cry out for His help!

Ephesians 4:26-27
"Do not let the sun go down while you are still angry, and do not give the devil a foothold."

Lord Jesus, heal the hurts that give birth to my anger and heal the hurts my anger has inflicted in others. In Your holy name I pray. Amen.

ONE
MINUTE
D E V O T I O N S

JUNE 20

By utilizing the discipline of journaling, I was finally able to understand why I was such an angry man. Some of my anger was the product of little hurts, carefully kept for years, which suddenly exploded in the most carnal ways. The issue that finally triggered my anger was usually a legitimate concern, but it was soon lost in the outpouring of my wrath. So what can we do? Realize some things aren't worth confronting and let them go. Others must be dealt with in love, firmly but without anger. Unresolved issues inevitably produce anger, so they cannot be ignored.

Proverbs 16:32
"Better a patient man than a warrior, a man who controls his temper than one who takes a city."

Lord Jesus, thank You for Your sanctifying work in me. Thank You that I am no longer the angry person I used to be. In Your holy name I pray. Amen.

ONE MINUTE
DEVOTIONS

JUNE 21

Keeping a prayer journal is important because we often have only a dim understanding of an experience or situation until we write it down. Once we put pen to paper our thoughts and feelings seem to crystallize, enabling us to present our true situation to God for healing and growth. As Robert Wood says, "Keeping a journal is the process of digesting the spiritual meaning of the events of each day."

Romans 12:2
"Do not conform any longer to the pattern of this world, but be transformed by the renewing of your mind."

Lord Jesus, help me to see things from Your perspective. Give me insight and understanding so I can live with integrity. In Your holy name I pray. Amen.

ONE MINUTE
DEVOTIONS

JUNE 22

God seldom makes His will known simply to satisfy our curiosity. More often than not, His Word comes as marching orders to the fully committed. That being the case, the first order of business is the unconditional surrender of our lives. Like Jesus in Gethsemane, we pray "…not my will, but yours be done" (Luke 22:42). Having surrendered ourselves to the plans and purposes of Christ, we can be confident that the Holy Spirit will guide us. We do not have to find the will of God. It will find us!

Psalm 138:8
"The LORD will fulfill his purpose for me."

Lord Jesus, I bring all my hopes and dreams and surrender them to You. Make Your will known to me that I may walk in obedience to Your plan for my life. In Your holy name I pray. Amen.

ONE MINUTE DEVOTIONS

JUNE 23

The best way to hear the voice of God is simply to be attentive when you pray. Pay attention when you worship. Be sensitive to the thoughts and impressions that come to you as you go about your duties. Pay special attention to any thoughts or impressions that are recurring. More often than not, God's guidance comes to us in the ordinary course of our lives.

1 Samuel 3:9
"If he calls you, say, 'Speak, LORD for your servant is listening.'"

Lord Jesus, give me a discerning ear that I may distinguish Your voice from all the other voices clamoring for my attention. And having discerned Your voice, give me faith to obey. In Your holy name I pray. Amen.

ONE MINUTE

DEVOTIONS

JUNE 24

How, you may be wondering, *can an ordinary person like myself hear God's voice?* Both Scripture and experience suggest that God usually speaks in one of four ways or some combination thereof. 1) Through the Scriptures. 2) Through the inner witness of the Holy Spirit. 3) Through providential circumstances and/or wise counsel. 4) Through special spiritual manifestations such as dreams and visions. Of this one thing you may be sure, God does speak, but it is up to us to discern His voice.

Acts 16:9-10
"During the night Paul had a vision of a man of Macedonia standing and begging him, 'Come over to Macedonia and help us.' After Paul had seen the vision, we got ready at once to leave for Macedonia, concluding that God had called us to preach the gospel to them."

Lord Jesus, help me to recognize Your voice however it comes to me. In Your Holy name I pray. Amen.

ONE
MINUTE
DEVOTIONS

JUNE 25

As I review the way the Lord has guided me through the years, three things stand out. 1) Obedience is mandatory. It does us little good to receive divine direction if we aren't willing to follow it. 2) God will give us wisdom for every situation. 3) We must step out in faith even when we don't know how things are going to turn out. Well it has been said, "God never gives us more light until we walk in the light we already have."

Psalm 37:23 KJV
"The steps of a good man are ordered by the Lord."

Lord Jesus, increase my faith that I may walk in obedience no matter how great the risk. In Your holy name I pray. Amen.

ONE
MINUTE
DEVOTIONS

JUNE 26

My experience suggests that God most often speaks in extraordinary ways when we are going to face unusual challenges in carrying out His directions. Knowing that Peter would be breaking the tradition of a lifetime, as well as risking the disapproval of his peers, God made His will emphatically clear through a vision and providential circumstances. Had His direction been any less dramatic, Peter might not have had the courage to take the gospel to the Gentiles at Cornelius' house.

Acts 11:12
"The Spirit told me to have no hesitation about going with them."

Lord Jesus, give me the faith and the courage to obey Your voice, even if it means risking the misunderstanding and disapproval of others. In Your holy name I pray. Amen.

ONE MINUTE
DEVOTIONS

JUNE 27

The spiritual leader who wants to keep his own ambition in check will submit his plans and visions to the judgment of a council of godly advisers. Spiritual guidance, whether it comes in the form of an inner witness or through a personal vision, is simply too subjective to be left to his judgment alone. If the spiritual leader's inner promptings are truly from the Lord, godly advisers will confirm them.

Proverbs 11:14 KJV
"Where no counsel is, the people fall: but in the multitude of counselors there is safety."

Lord Jesus, give me the grace to submit my plans and visions to the counsel of wise and godly advisers. In Your holy name I pray. Amen.

ONE MINUTE
DEVOTIONS

JUNE 28

The spiritual leader's counselors must be men of integrity. They must be strong enough to speak the truth in love and wise enough to discern between the wisdom of God and their own opinion. They should also provide an inner circle of spiritual support and protection for the man of God. In truth, almost all of us are our own worst enemy; therefore, every spiritual leader must surround himself with trustworthy people who will protect him from himself.

Proverbs 13:20
"He who walks with the wise grows wise, but a companion of fools suffers harm."

Lord Jesus, bring wise and godly people into my life. May they provide counsel and direction, lest I make foolish mistakes. In Your holy name I pray. Amen.

ONE MINUTE
DEVOTIONS

JUNE 29

The person who acts before God speaks is moving in presumption, not faith! The person who is walking in faith waits for God to speak and then obeys. God is the initiator. Faith is our obedient response. Presumption is man's attempt to force God to act on his behalf. Self seizes the initiative and takes action. The presumptuous person may think he is moving in faith, he may even be sincere, but this will not keep him from reaping the consequences of his rash action.

Matthew 4:7 KJV
"Jesus said unto him, It is written again, thou shalt not tempt the Lord thy God."

Lord Jesus, protect me from myself when ambition tempts me to be presumptuous, to attempt things You have not called me to do. In Your holy name I pray. Amen.

ONE MINUTE DEVOTIONS

JUNE 30

In a misdirected effort to motivate us to love one another, sincere people often make us feel responsible for the whole world and that is a burden too heavy to bear. In the final analysis the world is God's responsibility, not ours. I am not suggesting that we are not our brother's keeper, but only that our compassion must be tempered with wisdom. Only as we recognize and live within our limits will we know the joy of working as co-laborers with Him.

Matthew 11:28
"Come to me, all you who are weary and burdened, and I will give you rest."

Lord Jesus, help me to be passionately obedient, to do everything You have asked me to do and no more. In Your holy name I pray. Amen.

ONE MINUTE
DEVOTIONS

JULY 1

Jesus was often pressed on all sides. Everywhere He went, needy people mobbed him. To His credit He still managed to balance the work of ministry with both rest and worship, thus avoiding burnout. Not infrequently He withdrew from public ministry in order to renew His physical energies and restore His spiritual strength. It was not weakness, but wisdom that motivated Him to seek solitude for a season.

Matthew 14:13
"He withdrew by boat privately to a solitary place."

Lord Jesus, we all need to get away from time to time in order to renew our spiritual strength. Help me have the wisdom to go away so I can return refreshed and renewed. In Your holy name I pray. Amen.

ONE
MINUTE
DEVOTIONS

JULY 2

If Jesus needed to live a God-centered life rather than a need-centered one, if He needed to practice the rhythm of life in order to remain effective in ministry and fulfilled as a person, then it only stands to reason that we do also, only more so. The pace of contemporary life simply amplifies our need for that delicate balance between work, rest, worship, and play.

John 5:19
"I tell you the truth, the Son can do nothing by himself; he can do only what he sees his Father doing, because whatever the Father does the Son also does."

Lord Jesus, help me do only what You have called me to do—no more, but certainly no less. In Your holy name I pray. Amen.

ONE MINUTE
DEVOTIONS

JULY 3

In His infinite wisdom God designed the Sabbath to protect us from the dangers of physical exhaustion, psychological stress, and the interpersonal alienation that results from the idolization of work, including the work of ministry. "Six days do your work," He says, "but on the seventh day do not work, so that your ox and your donkey may rest and the slave born in your household, and the alien as well, may be refreshed" (Exodus 23:12).

Mark 2:27
"The Sabbath was made for man, not man for the Sabbath."

Lord Jesus, thank You for the gift of rest. Teach me to receive it with thanksgiving and to rest without guilt. In Your holy name I pray. Amen.

ONE MINUTE
DEVOTIONS

JULY 4

Don't deceive yourself. Rest is not optional. It can't wait! World War II ushered in the first widespread practice of seven-day-a-week, twenty-four-hour-a-day production. By the 1960's and the 1970's, retailers were following suit, and the Sabbath principle was a thing of the past. Not coincidentally, there was a significant increase in emotional dysfunction, juvenile delinquency, and divorce. Without the rhythm of rest provided by the Sabbath, life is unraveling at the seams.

———————————

Exodus 34:21
"Six days you shall labor, but on the seventh day you shall rest; even during the plowing season and harvest you must rest."

———————————

Lord Jesus, help me to give rest the same priority I give work. In Your holy name I pray. Amen.

ONE MINUTE
DEVOTIONS

JULY 5

In Old Testament times, Sabbath-breakers were executed. Exodus 35:2 says, "Whoever does any work on it [the Sabbath] must be put to death." Those who break the Sabbath today suffer similar consequences—not at the hands of a religious or judicial system, but as the inevitable consequence of their transgression. When you violate the Sabbath principle of rest, your soul suffers, as do your relationships, your creative energies, and, ultimately, your physical health.

Hebrew 4:9,11
*"There remains, then, a Sabbath-rest for the people of God.
Let us, therefore, make every effort to enter that rest."*

Lord Jesus, forgive me for working far too much in an attempt to prove my worth. Help me to trust Your grace and to enter into the rest You have provided. In Your holy name I pray. Amen.

ONE MINUTE
DEVOTIONS

JULY 6

Pausing for rest and renewal once a week simply isn't enough. If we are going to live the abundant life Jesus promised, we need to carry the spirit of the Sabbath into every day. In other words, every day should have something of the Sabbath in it—a time for rest, a time for relationships and a time for worship—but this won't just happen. We will have to carve out a place for these things in our busy day.

Isaiah 28:12 KJV
"This is the rest wherewith ye may cause the weary to rest; and this is the refreshing."

Lord Jesus, help me to pause in the midst of my hectic day and acknowledge Your presence and in Your presence may I find refreshing for my souls. In Your holy name I pray. Amen.

ONE MINUTE

DEVOTIONS

JULY 7

Without the Sabbath, without rest and renewal, we would never have the inner resources to embrace a hurting world. In our weariness we would be tempted to resent the needy with their ever-present claims on us, but renewed by a Sabbath of rest we can embrace them with the love of Christ. Rather than isolating us, the Sabbath empowers us; it restores our spiritual and emotional vitality so we can return to our mission with renewed vision.

Matthew 11:29-30 KJV
"Take my yoke upon you, and learn of me; for I am meek and lowly in heart: and ye shall find rest unto your souls. For my yoke is easy, and my burden is light."

Lord Jesus, give me rest and restore my soul so I can minister to others without burning out. In Your holy name I pray. Amen.

ONE MINUTE
DEVOTIONS

JULY 8

Perhaps we need to rethink our theology of worship. Maybe it is not just something that happens in the sanctuary. In fact, maybe what happens at church is really designed to sensitize us to God's presence in our everyday world. Fredrick Buechner says, "…church isn't the only place where the holy happens. Sacramental moments can occur at any moment, any place, and to anybody.…If we weren't blind as bats, we might see that life itself is sacramental."

Exodus 3:5
"Take off your sandals, for the place where you are standing is holy ground."

Lord Jesus, surprise me with a holy encounter in the midst of my work-a-day world. In Your holy name I pray. Amen.

ONE MINUTE DEVOTIONS

JULY 9

Has the Lord ever surprised you with an unexpected encounter in the midst of your busy day? It happened to me not long ago and like Jacob of old, I heard myself saying, "Surely the Lord is in this place, and I did not know it" (Genesis 28:16 NKJV). Like Moses standing barefoot before the burning bush or Elijah listening to that "still small voice," I knew I was standing on holy ground. For a minute, God met me in the midst of my busyness and when He did, it seemed He made all things new. My coffee had grown cold when I returned to my desk, but my heart was strangely warmed.

Acts 3:19 KJV
"The times of refreshing shall come from the presence of the Lord."

Lord Jesus, thank You for infusing my days with Your holy presence. In Your holy name I pray. Amen.

ONE MINUTE DEVOTIONS

JULY 10

It isn't easy to still my noisy heart or to quiet my anxious thoughts. But with determined deliberateness, I do the things that have worked in the past. I brew a cup of coffee. I light the kerosene lamp in my study. I force myself to sit and be still. Bit by bit I feel the tensions slip away. The noise of the world is pushed back for a little while. Even the discordant voices within grow quiet. Out of the silence, He speaks in a still small voice and my soul is renewed.

Revelation 2:11
"He who has an ear, let him hear what the Spirit says...."

Lord Jesus, help us to quiet the noisy voices within that we might hear Your still small voice. In Your holy name we pray. Amen.

July 11

Out of the silence, God speaks in a still small voice and my soul is renewed. There is no other way to say it—my soul is renewed. I know who I am—a child of God. I know who He is—my heavenly Father. Within the warmth of His embrace, within the comfort of His presence, my concerns, even my fears seem so inconsequential. The circumstances that caused them are still there, but they are no longer of any real concern "…for you are with me; your rod and your staff, they comfort me" (Psalm 23:4).

Psalm 94:19
"When anxiety was great within me, your consolation brought joy to my soul."

Lord Jesus, Your voice is my greatest comfort. When You speak the inner storms of doubt and fear cease. Blessed is Your holy name. Amen.

ONE MINUTE DEVOTIONS

JULY 12

Does your heart hunger for a life that is richer, more vivid, and fuller than before? If it does, let me urge you to make the rhythm of worship a part of your daily routine. It won't necessarily be easy, but it will be worth whatever effort it takes. As Anne Morrow Lindbergh writes, "I find there is a quality to being alone [with God] that is incredibly precious." Not only will you be renewed as a person, but you will also return to your daily life with a fresh anointing.

2 Corinthians 4:16
"Therefore we do not lose heart....(for) inwardly we are being renewed day by day."

Lord Jesus, I give You thanks for the daily bread that renews my soul, for the joy that comes from being shut in with God in a secret place. In Your holy name I pray. Amen.

ONE
MINUTE
DEVOTIONS

JULY 13

The disciplines that enable us to maintain our spiritual vitality, our emotional wholeness, and our physical strength include daily prayer, Scripture reading, fasting, meditation, solitude, and corporate worship. An equally important, but less recognized discipline is the rhythm of life—that delicate balance between work, rest, worship, and play. Without these spiritual disciplines, life's richness hangs by a slender thread.

1 Timothy 4:8
"For physical training is of some value, but godliness has value for all things, holding promise for both the present life and the life to come."

Lord Jesus, grant me physical strength, emotional wholeness, and spiritual vitality. In Your holy name I pray. Amen.

ONE MINUTE
DEVOTIONS

JULY 14

Life's richness flows out of its rhythm. Only a madman would try to plant in the dead of winter or harvest in seedtime. The fruitfulness of his labors depends on his willingness to work within the seasons of nature, within the rhythm of the land. By the same token, we live self-defeating lives when we ignore the divinely ordained rhythm of work, rest, worship, and play. To truly become all God has called us to be, we must live in rhythm with Him.

Ecclesiastes 3:1
"There is a time for everything, and a season for every activity under heaven."

Lord Jesus, teach me to balance my busyness with solitude, my work with rest. Let me walk away from time to time so I can return refreshed and renewed. In Your holy name I pray. Amen.

ONE MINUTE
DEVOTIONS

JULY 15

He who repeatedly chooses expediency over character will not have the moral strength to do what is right when the ultimate test comes. The man or woman who is determined to exercise integrity in the heat of crisis must practice it in the little matters that arise daily. In truth, the life-changing decisions we make in that moment are a foregone conclusion, the inevitable consequence of the choices we make every day, so choose wisely.

Proverbs 4:14
"Do not set foot on the path of the wicked or walk in the way of evil men."

Lord Jesus, protect me from the little snares, the temptations that seem inconsequential at the time, but which lead to moral failure in the heat of crisis. In Your holy name I pray. Amen.

ONE MINUTE DEVOTIONS

JULY 16

Jesus came to the cross as "the Lamb of God, who takes away the sin of the world" (John 1:29). He came as the Sinless One to suffer for sinful humanity, as the Righteous One to suffer for the unrighteous. But once the Roman soldiers nailed Him to the cross, a strange and terrible metamorphosis took place. The Lamb of God became a serpent (John 3:14) the Sinless One became sin itself (2 Corinthians 5:21) and God discharged on Him the full weight of His righteous judgment.

2 Corinthians 5:21
"God made him who had no sin to be sin for us, so that in him we might become the righteousness of God."

Lord Jesus, may I never forget that You suffered judgment at God's hand that I might live. May I never forget that You suffered the shame of the cross to deliver me from the shame of my sin. In Your holy name I pray. Amen.

ONE MINUTE
DEVOTIONS

JULY 17

When I was nine years old, Mother gave birth to our long-awaited baby sister. Unfortunately she was born hydrocephalic and only lived a few months. With a pain that lingers still, I remember watching as Mother gave Carolyn her daily bath. Next, she wrapped her in a pretty pink blanket and hugged her to her breast. A miracle happened then—not the one we had prayed for, not a miracle of healing, but a miracle of love. As Mother wrapped Carolyn Faye in the folds of her love and hugged her to her breast Carolyn was transformed. She was made lovely by our mother's love, at least to us.

1 Corinthians 13:8,7,13
"Love never fails…It always protects, always trusts, always hopes, always perseveres. And now these three remain: faith, hope and love. But the greatest of these is love."

Lord Jesus, may I never forget that Your love is all-powerful, transforming my brokenness into a thing of beauty. In Your holy name I pray. Amen.

ONE MINUTE DEVOTIONS

JULY 18

When we fall into sin, the enemy of our souls tries to convince us that God is ready to wash His hands of us, but that isn't true. Instead, we become the objects of His special loving attention. Like the good shepherd, Jesus leaves the ninety-nine and goes into the wasteland of sin searching for us. He doesn't give up when it gets dark or a storm blows up or it becomes dangerous or seems hopeless. No! He keeps searching until He finds us.

Luke 15:5-6
"And when he finds it, he joyfully puts it on his shoulders and goes home. Then he calls his friends and neighbors together and says, 'Rejoice with me; I have found my lost sheep.'"

Lord Jesus, thank You for never giving up on me no matter how far I may wonder or how great my sin. In Your holy name I pray. Amen.

ONE MINUTE
DEVOTIONS

JULY 19

If all we knew about the apostle Peter were his spiritual triumphs, he would be an intimidating figure indeed. By the same token, if all we knew of him were his failures, he would be forgettable at best—perhaps even tragic. But when we consider his spiritual achievements against the backdrop of his failures, we cannot help but be inspired. If God could use a man like Peter, then maybe, just maybe, He can use someone like us.

1 Corinthians 1:27
"God chose the weak things of the world to shame the strong."

Lord Jesus, I know that I am a flawed person with feet of clay. Still, I surrender myself to You believing that You can use even someone like me. In Your holy name I pray. Amen.

ONE MINUTE DEVOTIONS

JULY 20

What good intentions cannot do, what shame cannot do, what even the fear of eternal damnation cannot do, the unconditional love of Jesus does. Through all the weeks and months and years of our sinful wandering, He refuses to abandon us. His love will not let us go, and in the end it is His love that brings us back.

Jeremiah 31:3
"The Lord [says] 'I have loved you with an everlasting love; I have drawn you with loving kindness.'"

Lord Jesus, I pray for the wandering one, the one who has lost her way. Touch her with Your love and draw her to Yourself. Bring her home. In Your holy name I pray. Amen.

ONE MINUTE
DEVOTIONS

JULY 21

Many would like to accept Jesus as a prophet or a wise teacher, but they will not believe that He is the Son of God. Such an option is simply not viable. If Jesus is not the Son of God as He claimed, then only two options remain. Either He was a liar who falsely claimed to be divine or He was a madman suffering from delusions of grandeur. So who do you say Jesus is? Choose carefully, for what we believe about Jesus will determine our eternal destiny.

John 3:18
"Whoever does not believe stands condemned already because he has not believed in the name of God's one and only Son."

Lord Jesus, help me to lay aside my unbelief and declare, "You are the Christ, the Son of the living God." In Your holy name I pray. Amen.

ONE MINUTE
DEVOTIONS

JULY 22

Each act of spiritual obedience, no matter how small, reinforces the foundation of a person's spiritual character. Day by day he is strengthened with might through God's Spirit in the inner man (Ephesians 3:16). When a potentially overwhelming temptation arises he is prepared, for having been obedient in the face of seemingly insignificant temptations, he is now able to be obedient in the moment of crisis.

Hebrews 5:7
"During the days of Jesus' life on earth, he offered up prayers and petitions…and he was heard because of his reverent submission."

Lord Jesus, help me to be obedient in all things, both large and small, that I may be able to stand in the moment of crisis. May my walk ever be pleasing to You. In Your holy name I pray. Amen.

ONE MINUTE

DEVOTIONS

JULY 23

No matter what kind of mess you may have made of your life, God still loves you. Even if you are sure you have nothing to offer Him, God still wants you. Faith in yourself is not a prerequisite for salvation; only faith in Jesus Christ. If you can pray, "Lord remember me..." as the criminal dying on the cross beside Jesus did, Jesus will forgive your sins and save your soul.

1 Timothy 1:15
"Here is a trustworthy saying that deserves full acceptance: Christ Jesus came into the world to save sinners."

Lord Jesus, I believe You are God's only begotten Son and the only Savior of the world. I receive You as my Lord and Savior. In Your holy name I pray. Amen.

ONE MINUTE DEVOTIONS

JULY 24

Prayer is the primary vehicle through which God manifests His divine provision. When we fail to pray, we cut ourselves off from the resources of God. But when we pray, we align ourselves with the purposes of God. His unlimited power and resources are manifest in and through us for, "The prayer of a righteous man is powerful and effective" (James 5:16).

Ephesians 3:20
"Now to him who is able to do immeasurably more than all we ask or imagine, according to his power that is at work within us."

Lord Jesus, teach me to pray prayers that truly honor Your incalculable power and infinite resources. In Your Holy name I pray. Amen.

ONE MINUTE
DEVOTIONS

JULY 25

When trouble comes we do not despair; nor do we castigate ourselves for our lack of faith or berate ourselves for some imagined sin; neither do we blame God. Instead we simply acknowledge that as members of this human family we are subject to the inevitable storms of life. And because we know that "in all things God works for the good of those who love him" (Romans 8:28), we find strength in Christ, not only to endure trouble and hardship but to overcome it.

Psalm 34:17
"The righteous cry out, and the Lord hears them; he delivers them from all their troubles."

Lord Jesus, teach me to trust You no matter how severe the storm. Give me strength to endure. In Your holy name I pray. Amen.

ONE MINUTE
DEVOTIONS

JULY 26

If life is to be meaningful and fulfilling we must have a reason for living, something we believe in enough to die for it. William James, the noted psychologist said, "The only truly happy people I know are those who have found a cause to live for which is greater than themselves." For the apostle Paul that cause was Christ and he declared, "to live is Christ and to die is gain" (Philippians 1:21).

Acts 20:24
"I consider my life worth nothing to me, if only I may finish the race and complete the task the Lord Jesus has given me."

Lord Jesus, deliver me from the trap of living only for myself. Give me a reason for living, a holy obsession. In Your holy name I pray. Amen.

ONE MINUTE DEVOTIONS

JULY 27

Are you grieving a broken relationship, a failed marriage, or an estranged child? Don't lose hope. When all human efforts have failed, God is just getting started. Many a seemingly hopeless relationship has been restored through the persistent, passionate, even desperate prayers of a spouse or a parent who refused to give up. Coincidence? Hardly. Divine intervention? Absolutely!

Matthew 15:28
"Then Jesus answered, 'Woman, you have great faith! Your request is granted.' And her daughter was healed from that very hour."

Lord Jesus, do what we cannot do. Heal broken relationships and restore marriages and families. In Your holy name I pray. Amen.

ONE MINUTE
DEVOTIONS

JULY 28

As I recall my childhood, it is not the Little League baseball games I remember or the junior high football games, but the long summer evenings spent playing catch with my dad. Nor do I remember a single time when I gulped down a Big Mac on the way to a soccer game, but I do remember eating dinner as a family virtually every evening of my childhood. The rhythm of mealtime gave order to our daily lives while affording us an opportunity to connect with each other.

Ephesians 6:4
"Fathers, do not exasperate your children; instead, bring them up in the training and instruction of the Lord."

Lord Jesus, deliver me from my hectic lives. Help me to slow down and enjoy being a family. In Your holy name I pray. Amen.

ONE MINUTE DEVOTIONS

JULY 29

We are complex beings and our belonging needs can only be met through fellowship with God and a network of caring people. In relationship with God, we satisfy our heart's deepest hunger for spiritual intimacy. Through marriage and the family, we have the opportunity to develop the kind of relationships that meet our inborn need for emotional intimacy. Yet, for all of that, there is still a longing for a place to belong—an extended family, a community of believers where we can know and be known.

Ephesians 2:19
"You are no longer foreigners and aliens, but fellow citizens with God's people and members of God's household."

Lord Jesus, help my to satisfy my heart hunger for meaningful relationships by bonding with Your church in holy fellowship. In Your holy name I pray. Amen.

ONE
MINUTE
DEVOTIONS

JULY 30

As a discriminating reader, I value style nearly as much as substance and nothing frustrates me more than a poorly written book. In the margins of several books in my library I have written, "Lots of words but no music." I want to read books that sing. I want to feel, to laugh or cry, or even throw the book across the room in a fit of temper. In short, I want the books I read to move me in the deep places of my life.

Ecclesiastes 12:12
"Of making many books there is no end, and much study wearies the body."

Lord Jesus, sometimes I feel overwhelmed by all the information bombarding me. It wearies my mind without touching my soul. Speak to me in the deep places of my life. In your holy name I pray. Amen.

ONE MINUTE DEVOTIONS

JULY 31

Give yourself a treat. Get a tall latte with an extra shot of espresso, find a comfortable chair in a quiet place and open a good book. Let it speak to the deep places in your life, the places you've been too busy to examine. From time to time put your finger between the pages, forget about the things you've read, listen to your own life. Who knows, maybe by the time you've finished reading, you'll be renewed. A good book can do that, you know.

Psalm 23:1, 3
"The LORD is my shepherd...he restores my soul."

Lord Jesus, thank You for all the books You've used to restore my soul. Bless those who write them. In Your holy name I pray. Amen.

ONE MINUTE
DEVOTIONS

AUGUST 1

Does she grieve? Of course she does. Is she afraid? Sometimes. Especially when she thinks of her three grandchildren growing up without her, but she refuses to live in fear. If she had been given a choice, she would not have chosen divorce and cancer, but in the midst of it she has found strength in God and an appreciation for life unlike anything she has ever known. As a consequence she is joyously alive, howbeit in the face of great adversity.

2 Corinthians 1:9
"This happened that we might not rely on ourselves but on God, who raises the dead."

Lord Jesus, help me to seize the moment, to live every hour to the very fullest no matter how difficult my situation. In Your holy name I pray. Amen.

ONE MINUTE
DEVOTIONS

AUGUST 2

Life can be difficult and no one escapes its challenges. Sooner or later you will find yourself pressed to your limits. It may come in the form of a broken relationship, or unemployment, or a serious illness, or the death of a loved one. When it comes you will be tempted to define your life by that painful experience. Don't succumb to that temptation. Refuse to define your life by any single event, whatever it may be. It is a real part of your life, but that is all—just a part.

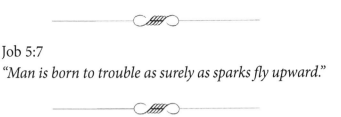

Job 5:7
"Man is born to trouble as surely as sparks fly upward."

Lord Jesus, help me to put each life experience—good and bad—into the context of my whole life. Touch and redeem each experience, be present in all of life. In Your holy name I pray. Amen.

ONE
MINUTE
DEVOTIONS

AUGUST 3

L ike a slide projected on the screen of my mind, I see an image of Mary. Her face is a suffering mask and I cannot even imagine what it must have been like for her. How does a mother watch her son being nailed to a cross? How does she bear it? Suddenly I have another thought. Mary wasn't the only one who had a son die that fateful day. Jesus was the Son of God as well as Mary's son. What was it like for Him? What did Father God feel as He watched His Son die?

Romans 5:8
"God demonstrates his own love for us in this: While we were still sinners, Christ died for us."

Father God, thank You for Your great love and Your incredible grace. I want to repay You somehow, but in my spirit I hear You say, "My love is not to be paid back but passed on." Help me to pass it on. In Jesus' name I pray. Amen.

ONE MINUTE
DEVOTIONS

AUGUST 4

On the phone, Mom is gushing with childlike enthusiasm. Their motel room has a small table where she and Daddy can play Dominoes, and an in-room coffeemaker. After she bids me goodby I sit for a moment, holding the now silent telephone in my hand. I can't help smiling at her excitement. I've stayed in enough no-name motels to know that the best of them leave much to be desired. Yet, Mom is as excited as a child on Christmas morning and that's one of the things I love most about her.

Matthew 18:3
"I tell you the truth, unless you change and become like little children, you will never enter the kingdom of heaven."

Lord Jesus, deliver me from cynicism. Restore my childlike enthusiasm. In Your holy name I pray. Amen.

ONE MINUTE
DEVOTIONS

AUGUST 5

A pastoral colleague has been receiving radiation therapy for stage two cancer at MD Anderson Cancer Clinic in Houston, Texas. Although he is several hundred miles from home and away from his children, he remains faith-filled. In every email he tells us of the many patients and their families that he's been able to minister to. Under the most adverse circumstances, he radiates joy and a Christlike compassion that is an inspiration to all who know him.

Psalm 34:17
"The righteous cry out, and the LORD hears them; he delivers them from all their troubles."

Lord Jesus, give me grace like that so I can serve with joy regardless of the circumstances in which I find myself. In Your holy name I pray. Amen.

ONE MINUTE
DEVOTIONS

AUGUST 6

Take a moment now and examine your life. What God-given dreams has the Lord placed in your heart? I'm not talking about personal ambitions, but dreams birthed by the Spirit. Dr. Jim Horvath, a personal friend of mine, carried a God-given dream of ministering in the Philippines in his heart for nearly twenty years before the Lord brought it to fruition. Now he has one of the most effective evangelistic ministries to the islands. What God has done for Jim, He will do for you!

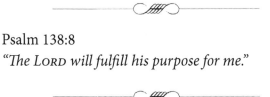

Psalm 138:8
"The LORD will fulfill his purpose for me."

Lord Jesus, I trust You with the dreams You have birthed in my heart. I believe You will bring them to fruition. In Your holy name I pray. Amen.

ONE MINUTE
DEVOTIONS

AUGUST 7

It is a mistake to make prosperity a goal. The Scriptures clearly teach that prosperity is a consequence, not a goal. The reason the Bible is filled with so many verses about divine provision is not to make us materialistic, but to assure us of the Father's abundant provision. He has repeatedly promised to take care of us so we don't need to concern ourselves about such things. We can focus our faith and our prayers on more important matters.

Matthew 6:33
"But seek first his kingdom and his righteousness, and all these things will be given to you as well."

Lord Jesus, teach me to pray for the coming of Your Kingdom and the doing of Your will on earth as it is in heaven. In Your holy name I pray. Amen.

ONE MINUTE
DEVOTIONS

AUGUST 8

Years ago, I found myself weeping as I sat alone with Mom in a small hospital room. Picking up one of her limp hands, I held it while tracing the purple veins on the back of her hand with my finger. She was comatose, the result of a brain aneurysm. I hated what had happened to her and I hated the thought of living in a world where she was no longer present. I couldn't help thinking that when she died I would lose the one person who always believed in me. Even when she knew the worst about me she always believed the best!

Proverbs 31:28-29
"Her children arise and call her blessed…Many women do noble things but you surpass them all."

Lord Jesus, help me to pass such spiritual values on to my children and grandchildren. In Your holy name I pray. Amen.

ONE MINUTE DEVOTIONS

AUGUST 9

With bated breath, the crowd watched the highwire artist make his torturous journey across Niagara Falls on a tightrope while pushing a wheelbarrow. As he prepared for his return trip he asked, "Do you believe I can do it with a man in the wheelbarrow?" With a single voice they shouted, "You can do it!" Yet when he asked for a volunteer to ride in the wheelbarrow, not a single person stepped forward. It was soon apparent that while no one doubted that he could do it, neither did anyone trust him enough to get in the wheelbarrow.

Proverbs 3:5
"Trust in the Lord with all your heart and lean not on your own understanding."

Lord Jesus, teach me to trust You with the little things that I might have the courage to trust You with the really important things. In Your Holy name I pray. Amen.

ONE
MINUTE
DEVOTIONS

AUGUST 10

Even the most cursory perusal of "Christian" television will reveal an inordinate emphasis on prosperity. Should you happen to tune in during one of the annual Share-A-Thons, that's virtually all you will hear. Apparently it is the most effective way to get viewers to give. Promise them a "hundred-fold" return and the phone lines light up. The question I am wrestling with is not whether it works or not, but is it Christian? Or to put it another way, is material prosperity a legitimate spiritual goal?

1 Timothy 6:11
"But you, man of God, flee from all this, and pursue righteousness, godliness, faith, love, endurance and gentleness."

Lord Jesus, forgive us for making material prosperity a goal. Deliver me from the seductive power of materialism. In Your holy name I pray. Amen.

ONE MINUTE DEVOTIONS

AUGUST 11

Brenda was weeping as we drove away from our cabin on Beaver Lake to assume our duties as pastors of Gateway Church in Shreveport. Turning to me she asked, "Why aren't you crying?" Gently I replied, "You're grieving what we are leaving while I'm looking forward to what lies ahead." Are you looking back, grieving what you have lost or are you looking ahead in faith, anticipating what God is going to do?

Genesis 19:26
"But Lot's wife looked back, and she became a pillar of salt."

Lord Jesus, grant me the courage and the faith to embrace the future that You have prepared, regardless of what it may be. In Your holy name I pray. Amen.

ONE MINUTE

DEVOTIONS

AUGUST 12

Speaking at our father's funeral, my brother said, "When Daddy took his last breath I knew I had lost an irreplaceable part of myself. The man who gave me life was gone and it felt like I had a hole in my heart. On another level, I knew Daddy was more alive than he had ever been and even as I wept with grief, I rejoiced. With the eye of faith I saw Daddy getting his passport stamped at heaven's gate. I could almost hear Jesus say, 'Welcome home, Dick Exley, welcome home!'"

Matthew 25:21 KJV
"Well done, thou good and faithful servant...enter thou into the joy of thy lord."

Lord Jesus, thank You for the promise of eternal life and a heavenly reward. In Your holy name I pray. Amen.

ONE MINUTE DEVOTIONS

AUGUST 13

We may legislate no-fault divorce laws and no-fault insurance laws, but there is no such thing as no-fault living. Every action has a consequence and as society has moved away from biblical values and traditional morality, we have seen a corresponding increase in divorce, dysfunctional families, sexually transmitted diseases, mental illness, and violent crime. This did not happen overnight and it will not be reversed in a single generation. Our only hope is a spiritual awaking that transforms humanity and returns our society to biblical values and traditional morality.

Romans 14:7
"For none of us lives to himself alone and none of us dies to himself alone."

Lord Jesus, help me to live a morally responsible life that I might build healthy relationships and a stable society. In Your holy name I pray. Amen.

ONE MINUTE DEVOTIONS

AUGUST 14

The rampant consumerism of the twenty-first century is unparalleled in the history of mankind. People live in huge houses with three car garages but have to park their cars in the driveway because their garages are overflowing with things they can't get in the house. Our addiction to things is further evidenced by the fact that one of the fastest growing businesses in the United States is storage rental. More and more people are renting off-site storage to store all the things they "own" and for which they have no place and often no use.

Luke 12:15
"Watch out! Be on your guard against all kinds of greed; a man's life does not consist in the abundance of his possessions."

Lord Jesus, deliver me from my obsession with things. In Your holy name I pray. Amen.

ONE MINUTE
DEVOTIONS

AUGUST 15

When a child dies, it often sounds the death knell for the marriage. Not so for my parents. Although their grief was unspeakable, it did not drive them apart. Instead they clung to each other, finding strength in their love. Years later I asked Mother how she made it after Carolyn died. Without a moment's hesitation she replied, "I had your father to help me. He listened when I needed to talk and when my grief was too deep for words, he held me."

Proverbs 12:18
"The tongue of the wise brings healing."

Lord Jesus, give me comforting words when others hurt and when they have no words, may my presence minister. In Your holy name I pray. Amen.

ONE
MINUTE
DEVOTIONS

AUGUST 16

In Herman Melville's *Moby Dick*, there's a turbulent scene in which a whaleboat pursues the great white whale. The sailors are laboring fiercely. The cosmic conflict between good and evil is joined—chaotic sea and demonic sea monster versus a morally outraged man, Captain Ahab. In this boat, though, there is one man who does nothing. He's the harpooner. Quiet, poised, waiting. And then this sentence: "To ensure the greatest efficiency of the dart, the harpooners of this world must start to their feet out of idleness and not out of toil."

Psalm 131:3
"Put your hope in the LORD both now and forevermore."

Lord Jesus, help me to live and minister out of a quiet confidence in Your sufficiency rather than out of a desperate franticness as if everything depended on me. In Your holy name I pray. Amen.

ONE MINUTE
DEVOTIONS

AUGUST 17

Choose to forgive the people who have betrayed you. By forgiving, you refuse to allow this tragedy to destroy you or your family. Even when God has intervened in a special healing way, you still have to choose to walk in your healing everyday. The enemy will continue to attack your mind and emotions. With the help of the Holy Spirit, discipline yourself to bring every thought into captivity to Jesus Christ (2 Corinthians 10:3-5).

2 Corinthians 10:4-5 KJV
"(For the weapons of our warfare are not carnal, but mighty through God to the pulling down of strongholds;) Casting down imaginations…and bringing into captivity every thought to the obedience of Christ."

Lord Jesus, enable me to walk daily in the spiritual and emotional healing You have wrought in me. In Your holy name I pray. Amen.

ONE MINUTE
DEVOTIONS

AUGUST 18

I couldn't help thinking how different Ray and Patsy were from the rest of our congregation. Christian Chapel was a "yuppie" congregation and they looked like homeless people—he with his bad teeth, out of style double-knit slacks, and scuffed shoes and she in her too small Salvation Army thrift shop dresses and taped-up glasses. In spite of this they seemed unaware of the vast social chasm that separated them from the other parishioners and worshipped Jesus with a joy that was pure and simple.

James 2:5
"Has not God chosen those who are poor in the eyes of the world to be rich in faith and to inherit the kingdom?"

Lord Jesus, help me to treat all people equally, rich and poor alike. May I always have room in my heart and in my life for the Rays and Patsys of this world. In Your holy name I pray. Amen.

ONE MINUTE
DEVOTIONS

AUGUST 19

We are literally working ourselves to death to possess things for which we have no use in order to impress people we don't even like. We use about 20 percent of our possessions, but we maintain 100 percent of them. That's the danger of materialism. You start out owning things, but before long they end up owning you! Sometimes it gets so bad that you can't give up a single thing, not even to save your soul. The only way to combat this ever-expanding consumerism is to deliberately buy less and give more away.

1 Timothy 6:9, 6
"People who want to get rich fall into temptation...But godliness with contentment is great gain."

Lord Jesus, teach me to be thankful for what I have rather than always wanting more. In Your holy name I pray. Amen.

ONE MINUTE DEVOTIONS

AUGUST 20

Not long ago someone told me that there are only two kinds of marriages: bad marriages and hard marriages. At first I was offended. But then I thought about it and decided he was right. Brenda and I have a good marriage and you can too, but it will take hard work. God gives us each other, the gift of love, and the covenant of marriage, but it is up to us to work the soil of our relationship all the days of our lives. And that is hard work!

Proverbs 19:14
"Houses and wealth are inherited from parents, but a prudent wife is from the Lord."

Lord Jesus, thank You for the gift of marriage. Help me to work at my marriage each and every day. In Your holy name I pray. Amen.

ONE MINUTE
DEVOTIONS

AUGUST 21

While we have a responsibility to discharge our duties as conscientious citizens, we must never put our hope in a candidate or a political party. God is our only hope and ultimately, only He can make society as it should be—a society where all people are created equal and love always triumphs over evil; a society where men will live by faith and not fear; a society where His Kingdom has been established and His will is being done on earth as it is in heaven.

Daniel 7:27
"His kingdom will be an everlasting kingdom, and all rulers will worship and obey him."

Lord Jesus, I pray for the coming of Your kingdom and the doing of Your will on earth as it is in heaven. In Your holy name I pray. Amen.

ONE MINUTE
DEVOTIONS

AUGUST 22

More than anything, God wants a relationship with you. That's why He sent His only begotten Son into the world. Not to condemn the world but that through Him the world might be saved. Unfortunately, many of us have created a religion of rules. But you can never know God by keeping the rules. The way to know God is relationally, the way a child knows his parents. So let God love you.

Isaiah 49:15
"Can a mother forget the baby at her breast and have no compassion on the child she has borne? Though she may forget, I will not forget you!"

Father God, teach me to relate to You as a trusting child relates to his loving father. In Jesus' name I pray. Amen.

ONE
MINUTE
DEVOTIONS

AUGUST 23

In today's political climate, ideological differences turn neighbors into enemies and truth is trampled underfoot in the rush to judgment. Is it too much of a stretch to suggest that such venomous emotions were the tinder that fuel -ed genocide in places like Kosovo and Rwanda? I think not. Given the current level of anger, we are in danger of becoming a monster in an attempt to destroy a monster. Without a return to civility in our public discourse, I fear anger may well escalate into violence right here in the United States.

Proverbs 15:1
"A gentle answer turns away wrath, but a harsh word stirs up anger."

Lord Jesus, may we be men and women of strong convictions but even stronger love. In Your holy name I pray. Amen.

ONE MINUTE DEVOTIONS

AUGUST 24

Regardless of what political party is in power, our responsibilities as Christ followers remain the same. The Scriptures command us to pray for our elected officials (1 Timothy 2:1-2), to act justly (Micah 6:8), to look after the orphans and widows (James 1:27), to make disciples (Matthew 28:19), to love God with our whole heart and our neighbor as ourself (Matthew 22:38-39) and to keep ourselves from being polluted by the world (James 1:27). As Christians we have a dual citizenship. While our highest allegiance belongs to God, we also have civic responsibilities that we owe the country of our birth.

Matthew 22:21
"Render therefore unto Caesar the things which are Caesar's; and unto God the things that are God's."

Lord Jesus, help me to live responsibly as a citizen of this world and the next. In Your holy name I pray. Amen.

ONE MINUTE
DEVOTIONS

AUGUST 25

So what is the worst thing you ever did? What is the one thing you hope no one ever finds out about you? When you have that evil deed fixed in your mind, I want you to ask yourself if God can forgive you. David says, "[God] does not treat us as our sins deserve or repay us according to our iniquities. For as high as the heavens are above the earth, so great is his love for those who fear him; as far as the east is from the west, so far has he removed our transgressions from us" (Psalm 103:10-12).

Jeremiah 31:34
"For I will forgive their wickedness and will remember their sins no more."

Lord Jesus, may I ever remember that Your grace is greater than my sin; that You are always more ready to forgive us than I am to receive Your forgiveness. In Your holy name I pray. Amen.

ONE MINUTE
DEVOTIONS

AUGUST 26

It embarrasses me to admit that there have been seasons in my life when I was so full of myself that there was no room for anyone else. Still, the Lord refused to give up on me. Patiently He worked with me, chipping away at my self-centered pride year, after year, after year, until, at last, something of His likeness began to rub off on me. Now I can truly rejoice with those who rejoice (at least most of the time), even if their achievements dwarf my own, which they almost always do.

Philippians 1:6
"He who began a good work in you will carry it on to completion until the day of Christ Jesus."

Lord Jesus, thank You for never giving up on me. In Your holy name I pray. Amen.

ONE MINUTE DEVOTIONS

AUGUST 27

I could read no further, so I put my finger between the pages and sat there with silent tears running down my cheeks. I was weeping for the author who couldn't weep for himself. I was weeping for the lonely drinker seeking relief in a bottle, the single parent struggling against all odds to make a normal life for herself and her children, and for the teenager who is shunned because she doesn't fit in. I was weeping for our broken world and I was weeping for myself.

Romans 12:15 KJV
"Rejoice with them that do rejoice, and weep with them that weep."

Lord Jesus, forgive me for closing my heart to those who are suffering. Move me to compassion. In Your holy name I pray. Amen.

ONE MINUTE
DEVOTIONS

AUGUST 28

On numerous occasions, I have witnessed God's healing love manifested through small groups of loving believers. The miracles are seldom instantaneous, but they are, nonetheless, dramatic. As one man testified, "The kindness of God and man made it possible for me to admit wrong and find healing and forgiveness….Though the experience is grueling, the reward is a life lived fully and actively before God and man, completely without fear."

Galatians 6:1
"Brothers, if someone is caught in a sin, you who are spiritual should restore him gently. But watch yourself, or you also may be tempted."

Lord Jesus, let Your healing, redemptive love shine through me. In Your holy name I pray. Amen.

ONE MINUTE
DEVOTIONS

AUGUST 29

Jesus lived as a common man among common men. He lived where they lived—fishermen, tax collectors, shepherds, street vendors—and He loved them all, outcasts of every kind, the untouchables, lepers, lunatics, Samaritans, street people, and women taken in adultery. He loved kids and crowds, celebrations and solitude, miracles and quiet meals with old friends. He was a blue-collar man and He calls us to be blue-collar Christians—loving the loveless and washing tired feet, even when there is no one to watch.

John 13:14-15
"Now that I, your Lord and Teacher, have washed your feet, you also should wash one another's feet. I have set you an example that you should do as I have done for you."

Lord Jesus, give me a true servant's heart and the strength to live it out. In Your holy name I pray. Amen.

ONE MINUTE
DEVOTIONS

AUGUST 30

Maybe you can't do much about economic exploitation or repressive political policies, but you can listen with love, lend a helping hand, share a meal, and speak an affirming word, and so can I. That may not seem like much, I mean it's not a cure-all for man's inhumanity to man, but if we can make just one person's load lighter, one person's dream a little brighter, if we dare to give into goodness now and then, then maybe, just maybe, someone else will be inspired to try goodness too, and who knows what might happen then.

Romans 12:21
"Do not be overcome by evil, but overcome evil with good."

Lord Jesus, help me to do small acts of kindness with great love. In Your holy name I pray. Amen.

ONE MINUTE
DEVOTIONS

AUGUST 31

A wise man once said, "When I was a young man, I admired clever men. Now that I am old, I admire kind men." I think I know what he meant. Clever people are generally self-centered and self-serving. They are quick to find the easy answer, the path of least resistance. They amuse the crowd with their quick wit, but they seem somehow to lack compassion. Kindness, on the other hand, wears well. Genuinely good men may not be flashy but over the long haul they always prove their worth.

Galatians 5:22-23
"But the fruit of the Spirit is love, joy, peace, patience, kindness…against such things there is no law."

Lord Jesus, help me to be a kind person, to think of others before I think of myself. In Your holy name I pray. Amen.

ONE MINUTE DEVOTIONS

SEPTEMBER 1

Sometimes the most significant thing we can do for the Kingdom of God is simply to encourage others. Only God knows how far-reaching our investment in their lives may be. When Barnabas took time to encourage Paul, I doubt he ever imagined that his kindness would affect believers for twenty-one centuries and beyond, but it did. Never make the mistake of belittling the eternal value of the encouragement and kindness you invest in another.

Proverbs 27:17
"As iron sharpens iron, so one man sharpens another."

Lord Jesus, thank You for those You have used to encourage me in my hour of weakness. Make me an encourager. In Your holy name I pray. Amen.

ONE MINUTE DEVOTIONS

SEPTEMBER 2

The late Dr. Karl Menninger of the Menninger Clinic concluded that most of his patients were hospitalized because they had not loved or been loved, or both. As a result, he called in his staff and told them that above all else they were to love. Every contact with patients was to be a love contact. From the top psychiatrists down to the electricians and window-cleaners, all were directed to express love toward the patients. Six months later, Dr. Menninger discovered that the expected hospitalization time of his patients had been cut by 50 percent.

1 Corinthians 13:13
"And now these three remain: faith, hope and love. But the greatest of these is love."

Lord Jesus, help me to receive Your unconditional love so I can love others unconditionally. In Your holy name I pray. Amen.

ONE MINUTE DEVOTIONS

SEPTEMBER 3

The tempter's ultimate goal is not simply to solicit our disobedience, but to discredit the character of God. Satan is pleased when he can lead us into sin, but that is a small thing compared to discrediting God. Sins can be forgiven, the wandering soul restored to fellowship, but if Satan can poison our hearts against God, we may be lost forever. To that end, he applies all of his evil genius.

2 Corinthians 2:11 KJV
"Lest Satan should get an advantage of us: for we are not ignorant of his devices."

Lord Jesus, protect me from the lies of the devil lest he distort the truth about God and poison my hearts and mind. In Your holy name I pray. Amen.

ONE MINUTE DEVOTIONS

SEPTEMBER 4

The Lord has given each of us gifts, special abilities. We can take no credit for them. It's like being seven feet tall—it isn't something over which we have any control. It's God's doing! While we cannot take credit for our gifts, we are responsible for them. We must discipline ourselves to fully develop our talents and we must use them responsibly to advance the Kingdom rather than just for our own benefit.

Luke 12:48
"From everyone who has been given much, much will be demanded; and from the one who has been entrusted with much, much more will be asked."

Lord Jesus, forgive me when I arrogantly flaunt my giftedness, taking credit for it and using it to draw attention to myself. Forgive me when I act irresponsibly, not using my gifts for the Kingdom. In Your holy name I pray. Amen.

ONE MINUTE
DEVOTIONS

SEPTEMBER 5

Ben's sister needed a kidney transplant and he was a possible donor. After much prayer he concluded that he had no right to live with two kidneys when his sister was facing death unless she had a transplant. He could have opted to let someone else serve as donor. He could have encouraged her to seek a cadaver kidney. But he didn't. Love wouldn't allow it—his love for his sister and his love for God.

Proverbs 3:27
"Do not withhold good from those who deserve it, when it is in your power to act."

Lord Jesus, give me a self-sacrificing love for others, a hurting family member, a brother or sister in Christ, or even the homeless stranger on the street. In Your holy name I pray. Amen.

ONE MINUTE

DEVOTIONS

SEPTEMBER 6

For eighteen months, John and his wife lived with death as their seven-year-old daughter battled leukemia. It was a roller coaster ride of highs and lows: periods of remission when hope was as exhilarating as the first barefoot day of spring, followed by a major relapse when hope was shattered on the rocks of reality. Finally death won, or so it seemed. Laura Lue died in her own bed, in her own room, as the snow fell softly outside her window.

John 11:25
"Jesus said to her, 'I am the resurrection and the life. He who believes in me will live, even though he dies.'"

Lord Jesus, I pray for all the children who are battling life-threatening diseases and for their parents. Be very near to them, hold them close to Your heart. In Your holy name I pray. Amen.

ONE MINUTE DEVOTIONS

SEPTEMBER 7

All of us have things in our past that we are ashamed of. "Things," that according to Paul Tournier, "we should like to blot out, things for which we feel ourselves responsible." Yet our only hope, our only path to freedom, is not in denying our past, shameful though it may be, but in honest confession. Although it is potentially a frightening experience, it is also liberating. Freed from the need to pretend to be someone we are not, we can finally be our real selves.

James 5:16
"Therefore confess your sins to each other and pray for each other so that you may be healed."

Lord Jesus, give me the courage to own my past and in this owning up, let me find forgiveness and freedom. In Your holy name I pray. Amen.

SEPTEMBER 8

A relationship seldom achieves its full potential without confrontation; but confrontation is almost always doomed to failure unless it grows out of a deep trust built on honest communication. Even then, it must be handled with sensitivity. If your friend is not convinced of your genuine concern, if he is not certain that you have his best interests at heart, he will likely become defensive, rejecting your correction.

Proverbs 12:18
"Reckless words pierce like a sword, but the tongue of the wise brings healing."

Lord Jesus, give me grace to bring correction when it is needed. Let my words be richly seasoned with love. In Your holy name I pray. Amen.

ONE MINUTE
DEVOTIONS

SEPTEMBER 9

"Self-knowledge," according to John Gardener, "is ruled out for most people by the increasingly effective self-deception they practice as they grow older." By middle age, most of us have learned to edit the truth about ourselves until it is more to our liking. The "facts" remain the same but the conclusions are totally different. We have mastered the art of self-deception and the lie we tell ourselves becomes the "truth" we tell others.

Jeremiah 17:9
"The heart is deceitful above all things and beyond cure. Who can understand it?"

Lord Jesus, don't let me get away with protesting my innocence or other self-justifying logic. Confront me with truth in the depth of my soul that I may be freed from self-deception. In Your holy name I pray. Amen.

ONE MINUTE DEVOTIONS

SEPTEMBER 10

Childhood memories, whether good or bad, shape who we become as adults. For instance, my father was an avid reader and I am told that when I was just a baby I would sit in his lap for hours, perfectly still, while he read. Thinking about it now, I realize that my love for books may well have been born right there in his arms. Even today I think of a good book as a trusted friend, and I associate them with happiness and love.

Psalm 77:11-12
"I will remember the deeds of the LORD; yes, I will remember your miracles of long ago."

Lord Jesus, thank You for the good memories that enrich my life and make me who I am today. In Your holy name I pray. Amen.

ONE MINUTE
DEVOTIONS

SEPTEMBER 11

I once ministered to a tragically tormented young woman. Although she was strikingly attractive and gifted, she lived with an overwhelming sense of worthlessness. It permeated her personality, colored her perception of life and undermined all of her relationships. The root cause of this deeply ingrained feeling and all the tragedies it birthed—three divorces, psychiatric treatment, and several suicide attempts —was a haunting childhood memory. It tormented her constantly, telling her that she was unloved and unwanted. But it doesn't have to be that way. Jesus can heal our memories.

Philippians 3:9,13 KJV
"And be found in him, not having mine own righteousness…[but]the righteousness which is of God by faith … forgetting those things which are behind, and reaching forth unto those things which are before…"

Lord Jesus, deliver me from my painful past with its tormenting memories. Give me a new life in Christ. In Your holy name I pray. Amen.

ONE MINUTE
DEVOTIONS

SEPTEMBER 12

After more than four decades in active ministry, my enthusiasm is undiminished. I'm not tired or burned out or discouraged. In fact, I love ministry more today than ever before. As long as God gives me strength, I plan to walk through every door He opens and do everything He calls me to do. I'm not looking for a place to stop, just for wisdom and guidance to do all the Lord puts before me!

Joshua 14:11
"I am still as strong today as the day Moses sent me out; I'm just as vigorous to go out to battle now as I was then."

Lord Jesus, thank You for physical strength and spiritual vitality to do the work of the ministry. In Your holy name I pray. Amen.

ONE MINUTE DEVOTIONS

SEPTEMBER 13

David Hogg taught a small Sunday school class of young boys. Out from that class went a young man, David Livingston, to Africa to walk out his life in missionary service. Some years later another missionary came to one of the same villages where Livingston had been. He told of the life and ministry of Jesus Christ. An old lady interrupted him, "That man has been here!" Think of it: a village church in Scotland; a consecrated Sunday school teacher; a little boy; and you get the footprints of Christ in and out of the muddy villages of Africa.

Matthew 25:23
"You have been faithful with a few things; I will put you in charge of many things."

Lord Jesus, help me remember that without David Hogg, there might not have been a David Livingston. In Your holy name I pray. Amen.

ONE MINUTE
DEVOTIONS

SEPTEMBER 14

Failure hurts! It's disappointing, embarrassing, humiliating. Say anything you want about its benefits, say it builds character, say it teaches us compassion; it still hurts. That is not to say that the benefits are not real, for they are, but it still hurts. Failure can contribute significantly to personal development, but that does not nullify the pain. It redeems it, gives it a noble purpose, but it does not eliminate it. Any way you cut it, failure hurts!

Proverbs 24:16
"For though a righteous man falls seven times, he rises again."

Lord Jesus, redeem my painful failures, I pray. Turn them into learning experiences. Use them to equip me for life and ministry. In Your holy name I pray. Amen.

ONE MINUTE
DEVOTIONS

SEPTEMBER 15

Tenderness is the touch of a mother's hand on the fevered brow of a sick child. It's her husband's quiet presence in the sick room; his strong arm around her trembling shoulder, his faith expressed in wordless prayer. It's a handwritten note from one who understands, a special scripture, a phone call. Tenderness is a shoulder to cry on in the hour of unspeakable loss. A friend who gives you time and a safe place to grieve, who comforts without resorting to clichés. Tenderness is God's presence expressed in human form.

2 Corinthians 7:6
"But God who comforts the downcast, comforted us by the coming of Titus."

Lord Jesus, make me a "Titus" to some lonely, hurting person today. In Your holy name I pray. Amen.

ONE MINUTE
DEVOTIONS

SEPTEMBER 16

The ministry of comfort is especially hard for men. It's hard for a man to sit and wait; to watch, powerless, as death does its dirty work. A man wants to do something, anything. He wants to exert his authority, regain control of his world, but that's not possible. He often ends up pretending the one he loves isn't dying. That may provide a temporary reprieve, but it cannot long protect him. In the end, only the presence of Jesus can sustain him in the dark hour of his grief.

Psalm 23:4
"Even though I walk through the valley of the shadow of death, I will fear no evil, for you are with me."

Lord Jesus, comfort me with Your presence and with the promise of eternal life. In Your holy name I pray. Amen.

ONE MINUTE DEVOTIONS

SEPTEMBER 17

Although it is nearly impossible for us to admit it, most of the trouble in our lives is of our own making. Denying that may be less painful in the short run, but in the end we pay a terrible price. As long as we blame someone else, we cut ourselves off from the grace of God that forgives and heals. We are able to get on with our lives only when we stop blaming others, take responsibility for our actions, and confess our sins.

Psalm 32:1
"Blessed is he whose transgressions are forgiven, whose sins are covered."

Lord Jesus, it is my fault. I have sinned against You and those I love most. Forgive me. Remember not the sins of my youth and my rebellious ways. In Your holy name I pray. Amen.

ONE MINUTE DEVOTIONS

SEPTEMBER 18

The guests varied from week to week but we almost never ate Sunday dinner alone. We might scrimp all week, as Mom used to say, but on Sundays we always had a feast. When we couldn't possibly eat another bite, we kids disappeared outdoors, while the adults lingered around the table talking for an hour or two. That's all they did—just talked. At the time, it seemed like such a waste to me. Now, I know better. That kind of talking nourishes the soul and reaffirms our place in the world.

Proverbs 10:11,21
"The mouth of the righteous is a fountain of life... The lips of the righteous nourish many."

Lord Jesus, thank You for good friends who speak into my life and for fellowship that nourishes my soul. In Your holy name I pray. Amen.

ONE MINUTE
DEVOTIONS

SEPTEMBER 19

Few things in life are more painful than a broken relationship. If you've lived for any length of time, I need say nothing more. It is a universal pain; an inevitable consequence of our fallen condition. Yet by the same token, there is nothing, absolutely nothing, that can compare with the unspeakable gift of a friend restored. When he forgives me, I realize all is not lost. I have not ruined everything—wounded it, yes; but forgiveness gives us another chance. It is the kiss of God that makes all things new.

Psalm 6:9
"The Lord has heard my cry for mercy; the Lord accepts my prayer."

Lord Jesus, thank You for healing my broken relationship and for restoring my friend. In Your holy name I pray. Amen.

ONE MINUTE
DEVOTIONS

SEPTEMBER 20

Have you found yourself overreacting to the situations in your life, becoming angry or bursting into tears? The world is full of people just like you—people whose emotional responses are disproportionate to the events that triggered them. As embarrassing and painful as these outbursts may be, they can be redemptive too. The key is to invite the Holy Spirit to show you why such insignificant issues trigger so much emotion. Once He has revealed the root cause, invite the Lord Jesus to heal your wounded soul.

Psalm 118:14
"The LORD is my strength and my song; he has become my salvation."

Lord Jesus, deliver me from yesterday's hurts lest they ruin today. In Your holy name I pray. Amen.

ONE MINUTE
DEVOTIONS

SEPTEMBER 21

Music is a powerful medium, often bypassing the intellect to touch the heart. Having once touched the heart, however, it returns to capture the mind, infusing it with images that are nearly unforgettable. Years later it only takes a few bars of that nearly forgotten refrain to bring it all rushing back, nearly as real as the first time. That is what makes worship songs so powerful—they touch both the heart and mind and enable us to embrace God with both our emotions and our intellect.

Psalm 103:1
"Praise the Lord, O my soul; all my inmost being, praise his holy name."

Lord Jesus, thank You for music that touches me in the deepest part of my being, enabling me to worship You with my whole being. In Your holy name I pray. Amen.

ONE MINUTE
DEVOTIONS

SEPTEMBER 22

Most of us think of life as a race to run, a mountain to climb, a challenge to meet, or an obstacle to overcome. With grim determination we set out to do battle with the forces arrayed against us. Given that mindset, is it any wonder that while we may achieve success, we seldom experience fulfillment? To live with meaning, life must be seen as a gift from God to be received with thanksgiving and lived with joy.

Ecclesiastes 5:19
"...To accept his lot and be happy in his work – this is a gift of God."

Lord Jesus, don't let the world system and the hectic demands of living blind me to life's best. Remind me that life is found not in the accumulation of things but in the riches of my relationships with family and friends and most especially in our relationship with You. In Your holy name I pray. Amen.

ONE MINUTE DEVOTIONS

SEPTEMBER 23

Are you one of the millions incarcerated in the penitentiary of pain? Do you suffer in solitary confinement, isolated by hurts you can't even talk about? There is only one way out and it won't be easy. You will have to forgive the very person who has ravished your soul. Only forgiveness can unlock the door of your prison.

Colossians 3:13
"Forgive whatever grievances you may have against one another. Forgive as the Lord forgave you."

Lord Jesus, I do not have the strength or the desire to forgive those who have wrecked my life. Help me I pray. Empower me to do what I cannot do in my own strength. In Your holy name I pray. Amen.

ONE MINUTE
DEVOTIONS

SEPTEMBER 24

Life hasn't been easy. Bank failures, home foreclosures, and unemployment tempt us to despair. Nothing anyone has done thus far has been effective, which should make any thinking person skeptical. If history is any indication, we are in for even tougher times before things get better. In the difficult days ahead, disappointment and difficulty will tempt us to focus on the negative but we dare not. Only hope will sustain us and gratitude is the fuel that feeds it.

1 Timothy 6:17
"Put [your] hope in God, who richly provides us with everything for our enjoyment."

Lord Jesus, forgive me for trusting in riches and other material things for my security. Teach me to trust only You. In Your holy name I pray. Amen.

ONE MINUTE DEVOTIONS

SEPTEMBER 25

Scripture teaches us that children are a heritage of the Lord and when we become parents, God entrusts us with a sacred charge. Should we fail here, all of our other achievements will be somehow diminished; but with God's help we need not fail. With God's help we can love our children unconditionally, discipline them consistently, and train them in the nurture and admonition of the Lord.

Proverbs 22:6
"Train a child in the way he should go, and when he is old he will not turn from it."

Lord, thank You for the gift of children. Empower me to teach them Your ways that they may grow up to become men and women of God. In Your holy name I pray. Amen.

ONE MINUTE DEVOTIONS

SEPTEMBER 26

Recently a high profile minister resigned after confessing to having an inappropriate relationship with a member of the opposite sex. Unfortunately, he is just the latest in a long line of colleagues who have fallen prey to temptation and disqualified themselves for ministry, at least for a time. Of course it is not just ministers who are susceptible to sexual temptation, we all are. And no one is more vulnerable than the person who thinks it could never happen to him.

1 Corinthians 10:12
"So, if you think you are standing firm, be careful that you don't fall!"

Lord Jesus, temptation is never more alluring than when I keep my struggle secret. Give me the courage to make myself accountable. In Your holy name I pray. Amen.

ONE MINUTE DEVOTIONS

SEPTEMBER 27

Tough times are here, make no mistake about it. Millions are unemployed, businesses are failing, marriages are in trouble, and terminal illness stalks us all. I'm not being negative. I'm a realist and I've lived long enough to know that sooner or later tough times come to everyone. But that is not the end of the story. God is greater than any storm we will ever face and His grace is sufficient. We can live with meaning and purpose no matter our lot in life.

Joshua 1:9
"Have I not commanded you? Be strong and courageous. Do not be afraid; do not be discouraged, for the Lord your God will be with you wherever you go."

Lord Jesus, help me to trust You even if I cannot understand Your ways, for You are my only hope, my only help. In Your holy name I pray. Amen.

ONE MINUTE
DEVOTIONS

SEPTEMBER 28

It is comforting to think of God as our heavenly Father, good and merciful, gracious and kind, but it is not enough. Given the troubles many of us face, we need not only a heavenly Father who cares but also one who has the power to do something about our situation. One who can speak to the storms that are threatening to overwhelm us and command them to cease. One who can make every situation work for our eternal good.

Psalm 112:7-8
"They will have no fear of bad news; their hearts are steadfast, trusting in the LORD. Their hearts are secure, they will have no fear; in the end they will look in triumph on their foes."

Lord Jesus, help me to remain strong until You deliver me from all my troubles. In Your holy name I pray. Amen.

ONE MINUTE
DEVOTIONS

SEPTEMBER 29

Bruce Larson suggests that the "...neighborhood bar is possibly the best counterfeit there is to the fellowship Christ wants to give His church." He goes on to say, "The bar flourishes not because most people are alcoholics, but because God has put into the human heart the desire to know and be known to love and be loved, and so many seek a counterfeit at the price of a few beers."

Acts 2:44-46
"All the believers were together and had everything in common. They sold property and possessions to give to anyone who had need. Every day they continued to meet together in the temple courts. They broke bread in their homes and ate together with glad and sincere hearts."

Lord Jesus, help me to make room in my hectic life for friends and friendship. Teach me to care, listen, and love. In Your holy name I pray. Amen.

ONE
MINUTE
DEVOTIONS

SEPTEMBER 30

We are complex beings, and our belonging needs can be met only through fellowship with God and a network of loving people. In relationship with God we satisfy our hearts' deepest hunger for spiritual intimacy. Our need for emotional intimacy is met in loving family relationships. Yet, for all of that, we still long for something more, a place to belong, a place where we can know and be known, what the New Testament calls *koninea*.

1 John 1:3
"We proclaim to you what we have seen and heard, so that you also may have fellowship with us. And our fellowship is with the Father and with his Son, Jesus Christ."

Lord Jesus, my relationships are often superficial and unfulfilling. Give me the authentic relationships for which my heart hungers. In Your holy name I pray. Amen.

ONE MINUTE
DEVOTIONS

OCTOBER 1

When we succumb to temptation, we have a choice. We can deny our sin and pretend that we have not transgressed or we can confess our sins and trust God's unconditional love. Unfortunately, many of us know little or nothing of God's unconditional love and as a result we are trapped in our sin. Fear of rejection imprisons us and we distance ourselves from the very One who longs to forgive and restore us.

Jeremiah 31:3
"I have loved you with an everlasting love; I have drawn you with loving-kindness."

Lord Jesus, let me experience Your unconditional love, not as a dusty doctrine, but as a life-changing reality. In Your holy name I pray. Amen.

ONE MINUTE
DEVOTIONS

OCTOBER 2

As I prepare this devotion, my eyes are damp with tears and my heart hurts. In a recent four-year period death claimed four of the most important people in my life. Although my grief has been nearly unspeakable at times, it was richly seasoned with the promise of God's presence and the hope of eternal life. At last I have moved from grief to gratefulness, rather than grieving their deaths, I am now celebrating the rich lives they lived.

1 Thessalonians 4:13
"Brothers, we do not want you to be ignorant about those who fall asleep, or to grieve like the rest of men, who have no hope."

Lord Jesus, redeem my memories. Turn my grief into gratefulness that I may praise You all the days of my life. In Your holy name I pray. Amen.

ONE MINUTE DEVOTIONS

OCTOBER 3

I believe God is near even when I cannot sense His presence. I believe He loves me even when I act in the most sinful and unloving ways. I am amazed at His patience and His persistence, but I am thankful too! I am thankful that He is a very present help in the time of trouble and that He hears me when I call, no matter how far I may have wandered or how disobedient I may have been. I am thankful that whatever concerns me concerns Him.

Exodus 15:11

"Who among the gods is like you, O LORD? Who is like you – majestic in holiness, awesome in glory, working wonders?"

Lord Jesus, be nearer than the breath I breathe and closer than life itself. In Your holy name I pray. Amen.

ONE MINUTE
DEVOTIONS

OCTOBER 4

You can't always control your circumstances or what others think about you or how they treat you, but you can choose your attitude. You can complain about what you don't have or you can thank God for what you do have. The choice is yours. "Two men looked out through prison bars. One man saw the mud. One man saw the stars." So what are you going to be: a stargazer or a mud sucker? The choice is yours.

Psalm 146:1
"I will praise the LORD all my life; I will sing praise to my God as long as I live."

Lord Jesus, I choose to give You thanks, this day and every day. In Your holy name I pray. Amen.

ONE MINUTE DEVOTIONS

OCTOBER 5

After their children are grown and gone, many a parent realizes that for all of their good intentions, they have handicapped the children they love more than life. They have damaged them, not out of cruelty but out of kindness. By giving their children all they could ever need or want, they have deprived them of the very things God uses to make us into the men and women He has called us to be.

Romans 5:3-4
"We know that suffering produces perseverance; perseverance, character; and character, hope."

Lord Jesus, give me the strength to let my children endure hardship that You might develop character in them. In Your holy name I pray. Amen.

ONE MINUTE

D E V O T I O N S

OCTOBER 6

Although the crucifixion of Jesus appears to be a tragic miscarriage of justice, it was not. He was not a helpless victim, but a willing sacrifice. He chose to die so we could live. He endured the shame of the cross so that we do not have to bear the shame of our sin. He was made to be sin for us so that we might be made the righteousness of God in Him.

1 Peter 1:18-19
"It was not with perishable things such as silver or gold that you were redeemed...but with the precious blood of Christ, a lamb without blemish or defect."

Lord Jesus, help me to come and receive Your love so I can go share it with others. In Your holy name I pray. Amen.

ONE MINUTE
DEVOTIONS

OCTOBER 7

Let me speak to the men for a moment. If you are like most men, you probably have a number of associates but very few real friends. That shouldn't be surprising. From childhood, you have been taught to be competitive, to see associates as rivals rather than potential friends. As a result your relationships are generally superficial. Men do things together, we talk about politics, business, sports, even religion, but we don't share our feelings. Jonathan and David had a different kind of relationship, a relationship built on vulnerability and transparency. As a result their friendship remains the standard by which all friendships are measured.

1 Samuel 18:1
"Jonathan became one in spirit with David, and he loved him as himself."

Lord Jesus, help me to be part of a friendship like David had with Jonathan. Help me to be vulnerable and transparent in my relationships. In Your holy name I pray. Amen.

ONE MINUTE
DEVOTIONS

OCTOBER 8

Who knows what makes a man like Judas Iscariot do what he did. Of this we can be sure, he did not follow Jesus in order to betray him. Like the other disciples, he left everything—family, friends, career—to serve Him. Along the way something happened that poisoned his soul and made him susceptible to Satan's snare, some little thing most likely. Then according to the scriptures, "…Satan entered Judas, called Iscariot, one of the Twelve" (Luke 22:3).

Proverbs 4:23
"Above all else, guard your heart, for it is the wellspring of life."

Lord Jesus, help me to carefully guard my heart lest a root of bitterness poison my soul and give Satan a foothold in my life. In Your holy name I pray. Amen.

ONE MINUTE DEVOTIONS

OCTOBER 9

Knowing how headstrong I can be, I've developed a daily habit of laying all of my hopes, dreams, ambitions, and desires at the foot of the Cross. I give them to God while praying, "Lord Jesus, I give You permission to change my desires, to superimpose Your will on mine. Now guide me through my surrendered desires and fulfill Your purposes in my life."

Jeremiah 1:5
"Before I formed you in the womb I knew you, before you were born I set you apart."

Lord Jesus, reveal the plans and purposes You have for me through my surrendered desires that I may do Your will each day. In Your holy name I pray. Amen.

ONE MINUTE

DEVOTIONS

OCTOBER 10

Some years ago, a man came to my office for counseling. He chose to see me rather than his own pastor, so great was his shame. Hardly had I closed the office door before he fell to his knees sobbing. For several minutes he wept before the Lord. Finally he was able to compose himself and only then did he share his dark secret. "I've failed my family and my God," he confessed. "Is there any hope for me?"

Psalm 103:10,12
"[God] does not treat us as our sins deserve or repay us according to our iniquities. As far as the east is from the west, so far has he removed our transgressions from us."

Lord Jesus, forgive my willful sins and change me. Make me into the person You have called me to be. In Your holy name I pray. Amen.

ONE MINUTE DEVOTIONS

OCTOBER 11

The difference between sanctified ambition and human ambition is simple. Sanctified ambition originates in the heart of the Father and is fueled by a sincere desire to please Him; human ambition originates in the heart of man and is driven by his own ego needs. And herein lies a great danger to the man or woman of God—we are not tempted to do bad things as much as we are tempted to attempt things God has not called us to do in order to satisfy our own ego.

Psalm 119:10
"I seek you with all my heart; do not let me stray from your commands."

Lord Jesus, sanctify my ambition, redeem it, conform it to Your perfect will. In Your holy name I pray. Amen.

ONE MINUTE DEVOTIONS

OCTOBER 12

When called to confront controversial issues, most of us will be tempted to sacrifice personal integrity in a misguided attempt to maintain unity. Given our propensity to avoid conflict, it is important to remember that God values some things more than unity—things like obedience, truth and integrity. No matter how futile your efforts may appear, don't give up. I'm convinced that every action counts and our involvement makes a difference.

Psalm 119:5
"Oh, that my ways were steadfast in obeying your decrees!"

Lord Jesus, give me the courage to do what is right no matter the cost. And give me the grace to act in love, not anger. In Your holy name I pray. Amen.

ONE MINUTE
DEVOTIONS

OCTOBER 13

Misguided zeal undermines the work of the Lord in any number of ways. Not infrequently, it produces unrealistic expectations, which lead to devastating disappointment. When you have the wrong people doing the wrong things for the wrong reasons you end up with an aberration, a monument to a man, rather than a work that glorifies God. Let that person succumb to the excesses his zeal encourages, and no little damage is done to the body of Christ.

1 Samuel 15:12,22-23
"[Samuel] was told, 'Saul has gone to Carmel. There he has set up a monument in his own honor'....Samuel replied . . . Because you have rejected the word of the LORD, he has rejected you.'"

Lord Jesus, deliver me from misguided zeal. In Your holy name I pray. Amen.

ONE MINUTE DEVOTIONS

OCTOBER 14

It's easy to limit our Christian service to "spiritual" things. You know—Bible studies, choir, fellowship groups with "our kind of people." Nice things, safe things, which let us feel we are serving without running the risk of getting our hands dirty. It's a subtle trap, and one not easily discerned—a trap in which we mistake busyness for commitment, and religious activity for true spiritual activism.

Matthew 23:23
"Woe to you, teachers of the law and Pharisees, you hypocrites!...you have neglected the more important matters of the law—justice, mercy and faithfulness."

Lord Jesus, help me to be a spiritual activist serving others rather than a religious busybody. In Your holy name I pray. Amen.

ONE MINUTE
DEVOTIONS

OCTOBER 15

According to Frederick Buechner, a Presbyterian minister and best-selling author, "Compassion is the sometimes fatal capacity for feeling what it is like to live inside somebody else's skin. It is the knowledge that there can never really be any peace and joy for me until there is peace and joy finally for you too." With an attitude like that, it's virtually impossible to ignore a single cry for help.

Colossians 3:12
"Therefore, as God's chosen people, holy and dearly loved, clothe yourselves with compassion, kindness, humility, gentleness and patience."

Lord Jesus, give me a compassionate heart. Help me to care about others as much as I care about myself. In Your holy name I pray. Amen.

OCTOBER 16

As a young pastor, I fell prey to the most subtle of all temptations—pride. As a result I made some misguided decisions resulting in a period of failure and disappointment. Like Humpty Dumpty, I had a great fall and all the king's men could not put me back together again. But what the king's men couldn't do, the King's Son did—Jesus put this broken man back together again and restored me to ministry.

Luke 15:22-24
"But the father said, '...this son of mine was dead and is alive again; he was lost and is found.' So they began to celebrate."

Lord Jesus, I'm so thankful that Your grace is always greater than our sin and that Your love forgives and restores. In Your holy name I pray. Amen.

ONE MINUTE DEVOTIONS

OCTOBER 17

With an effort, she began to reminisce, to recall the love and the laughter they had shared. As she did, the awful pain of her grief gave way, just a little, to the joy of their shared past. She was still undone by the magnitude of her loss, but her grief was now tempered with memories of the good times they had shared. I'm not talking about denial, but perspective. Her loss is real, as is her grief, but so are the memories, and the sunshine, and God!

Philippians 4:7
"And the peace of God, which transcends all understanding, will guard your hearts and your minds in Christ Jesus."

Lord Jesus, help me to remember the joy of life no matter how deep the grief. In Your holy name I pray. Amen.

ONE MINUTE
DEVOTIONS

OCTOBER 18

Contented people have at least five characteristics in common. 1) They are committed to a cause greater than themselves. 2) They have a servant's heart. 3) They value relationships. They love people rather than things. 4) They give thanks for what they have rather than complaining about what they don't have. 5) They celebrate the ordinary, finding joy in life's little pleasures.

Nehemiah 8:10
"Nehemiah said, 'Go and enjoy choice food and sweet drinks, and send some to those who have nothing prepared. This day is holy to our Lord. Do not grieve, for the joy of the LORD is your strength.'"

Lord Jesus, teach me to love people not things and to live my life in loving service. In Your holy name I pray. Amen.

ONE MINUTE
DEVOTIONS

OCTOBER 19

In the world's economy, it is the movers and shakers who get things done. They take the bull by the horns and make things happen. In the economy of the Kingdom, the Word of God is supreme. We do only what He directs us to do. There is never a situation in which we can justify bending the rules in order to get the job done. Those who yield to the temptation to do things their own way court destruction, for it is only a small step from foolish independence to sinful disobedience.

1 Samuel 15:23
"For rebellion is like the sin of divination, and arrogance like the evil of idolatry."

Lord Jesus, protect me from my willful independence. Teach me to submit to Your will. In Your holy name I pray. Amen.

ONE MINUTE
DEVOTIONS

OCTOBER 20

I want to be like the little boy who asked his mother what his conscience was. She replied, "Conscience is that little voice inside of you that warns you when you are about to do something bad." At bedtime that night, the little fellow knelt beside his bed to pray. Folding his hands he prayed, "Dear God, please make my little voice loud."

Psalm 119:9-10
"How can a young man keep his way pure? By living according to your word. I seek you with all my heart; do not let me stray from your commands."

Lord Jesus, make me sensitive to the voice of Your Spirit and willing to obey. In Your holy name I pray. Amen.

ONE MINUTE DEVOTIONS

OCTOBER 21

I love the story of Jacob wrestling with God in the dark, on the muddy bank of the Jabbok. Finally he submits to the LORD and he is changed. God declares that Jacob has become Israel. The deceitful con man has become a prince. He's still not perfect (no one is in this life), but he is changed! And, as unbelievable as it may seem, limping Israel has a power with God and man that the self-reliant Jacob never had.

Genesis 32:30
"So Jacob called the place Peniel, saying, 'It is because I saw God face to face, and yet my life was spared.'"

Lord Jesus, wrestle with me in the dark night of my sinfulness until finally I submit to You. Change my as You changed Jacob. In Your holy name I pray. Amen.

ONE MINUTE

DEVOTIONS

OCTOBER 22

The importance of family is most evident in the dark hours immediately following a tragic accident or while battling a life-threatening illness. Years ago when our seemingly indestructible father underwent open-heart surgery, the strength of our lifelong family bonds stood us in good stead. We supported one another. We prayed together when praying alone was more than we could manage. And as Dad recovered, we filled his hospital room with the healing gift of laughter, recalling childhood pranks and family fun.

Genesis 50:1
"Joseph threw himself upon his father and wept over him and kissed him."

Lord Jesus, thank You for the gift of family, for the joy and strength it brings at all times, but especially when trouble strikes. In Your holy name I pray. Amen.

ONE MINUTE
DEVOTIONS

OCTOBER 23

Life is fleeting and I look back on our daughter's childhood with nostalgia, hardly able to believe how quickly it came and went. At least I have the memories. In the winter we went snowmobiling high in the Colorado Rockies or ice-skating in the park. In the summer we hiked and picnicked in the mountains. In the fall we cut firewood, buoyed by the prospect of long winter evenings in front of a roaring fire. Those special times didn't just happened though. We planned them and made family time a priority.

Psalm 127:3-4
"Children are a heritage from the Lord, offspring a reward from him. Like arrows in the hands of a warrior are children born in one's youth."

Lord Jesus, thank You for the gift of children and the joy they bring. May I always realize what a treasure they are. In Your holy name I pray. Amen.

ONE MINUTE
DEVOTIONS

OCTOBER 24

Sexual temptation is so powerful that unless a stake is driven into its heart immediately, it may well overwhelm us. Kings have renounced their thrones, saints their God, and spouses their lifetime partners. People have been known to sell their souls, jobs, reputations, children, and marriage—they have literally chucked everything for a brief moment of sexual pleasure. Guard your heart. Don't let it happen to you!

Proverbs 6:25-26
"Do not lust in your heart after her beauty or let her captivate you with her eyes, For the prostitute reduces you to a loaf of bread and the adulteress preys upon your very life."

Lord Jesus, teach me to recognize and heed the Holy Spirit's earliest warnings lest I fall prey to sexual sin. In Your holy name I pray. Amen.

ONE
MINUTE
DEVOTIONS

OCTOBER 25

Home groups, what many churches now call "Life Groups," are the relational heart of the local church, the core of New Testament community, and the answer to our social loneliness. They are an extended family. They give us a place to know and be known. They make New Testament fellowship a reality—even in our busy, impersonal world.

Acts 2:44,46
"All the believers were together… They broke bread in their homes and ate together with glad and sincere hearts."

Lord Jesus, help me to make my home a place of hospitality where I share food and fellowship with friends old and new. In Your holy name I pray. Amen.

ONE MINUTE DEVOTIONS

OCTOBER 26

When asked about his relationship to Jack Benny, George Burns replied, "Jack and I had a wonderful friendship for nearly fifty-five years. Jack never walked out on me when I sang a song, and I never walked out on him when he played the violin." Though couched in jest, Burns expressed the commitment that characterized their relationship. Hardly a day went by when they didn't talk, at least by telephone. Each would have done anything for the other.

1 Samuel 20:42
"Go in peace, for we have sworn friendship with each other in the name of the Lord*."*

Lord Jesus, thank You for those friends who have proven their faithfulness through the years. Help me to always be a faithful friend. In Your holy name I pray. Amen.

ONE MINUTE
DEVOTIONS

OCTOBER 27

Shelby is an overcomer. She writes, "Don't waste time and energy in being bitter over the bad deal you got in life. I have lived through sexual abuse as a child, desertion and divorce as an adult. I have experienced the death of my younger sister through cancer and my own serious hospitalization with typhoid fever. Yet I believe God wants me to use all of this to help others. He can't do this if I'm sitting in self-pity or anger."

Genesis 50:20
"You intended to harm me, but God intended it for good to accomplish what is now being done, the saving of many lives."

Lord Jesus, help me to trust You with my tragedies believing that You can turn them into material for ministry. In Your holy name I pray. Amen.

ONE MINUTE
DEVOTIONS

OCTOBER 28

Have you ever considered the healing power of a touch? A woman suffering from the ravishes of cancer said, "The greatest gift was touching. Friends sat beside me as I lay exhausted on our couch. They touched my shoulder, held my hand, kissed my cheek, hugged me; their touch cushioned me. At the hospital they washed and curled my hair, gave me manicures, and set guard duties so I could rest. When I grew exhausted, they read my Bible to me and jotted my personal correspondence."

Mark 16:18
"They will place their hands on sick people, and they will get well."

Lord Jesus, give me the grace to touch those who are sick and broken by life. In Your holy name I pray. Amen.

ONE MINUTE DEVOTIONS

OCTOBER 29

Recently I read a modern day prodigal's prayer. "Lord, here's my life, such as it is, a patchwork of small successes interlaced with repeated failures—an ordinary life, for the most part, used and sometimes misused, definitely in need of new management. Govern me, I pray, with Your holy love. Direct all the decisions of my life. Teach me to budget my limited resources of time and talent, lest I squander them foolishly on selfish goals and things that don't really matter."

Luke 15:17-18
"When he came to his senses, he said, '…I will set out and go back to my father and say to him: Father, I have sinned.'"

Lord Jesus, forgive my sinful failures and take over the management of my life. Make me the person I was called to be. In Your holy name I pray. Amen.

ONE MINUTE
DEVOTIONS

OCTOBER 30

The person who believes that God loves him as he is, with all of his "hang-ups," believes the unbelievable. Such love is beyond us, it's too good to be true. Now and then we catch a glimpse of it reflected through the selfless love of others. At other times it's just a feeling, a knowing that is too deep for words. And with that knowledge there comes a security, a confidence, that enables us to risk loving and living in ways we never dared before.

Romans 8:38-39
"For I am convinced that neither death nor life, neither angels nor demons, neither the present nor the future, nor any powers, neither height nor depth, nor anything else in all creation, will be able to separate us from the love of God that is in Christ Jesus our Lord."

Lord Jesus, help me to trust Your love more. In Your holy name I pray. Amen.

ONE MINUTE DEVOTIONS

OCTOBER 31

A few years ago, a pastor friend was diagnosed with inoperable cancer just before Thanksgiving. Following his diagnosis he wrote, "I am thankful for God who is real and personal, for a Christ who is present in power, and for the Holy Spirit who is by our side in every struggle… My Thanksgiving list this year is made not from what I have, but from Who has me—a God who is able to do exceedingly abundantly above all I ask or think."

Isaiah 41:13
"For I am the LORD YOUR GOD who takes hold of your right hand and says to you, Do not fear; I will help you."

Lord Jesus, I thank You for the promise of Your presence, the possibility of healing, and the hope of eternal life. In Your holy name I pray. Amen.

ONE MINUTE DEVOTIONS

NOVEMBER 1

Make no mistake. Taking responsibility for your actions is never easy. It's a choice—a tough choice, but a wise one. The prodigal made that choice. He did not plead bad luck, or a downturn in the economy, or even extenuating circumstance. He simply said, "Father, I have sinned against heaven and against you. I am no longer worthy to be called your son" (Luke 15:18-19). He returned home, seeking not pity but pardon, not understanding but mercy, and he was welcomed back into his father's house.

Luke 15:20 NKJV
"But when he was still a great way off, his father saw him and had compassion."

Lord Jesus, I trust not in my own merit but only in Your mercy to forgive and restore. In Your holy name I pray. Amen.

ONE MINUTE
DEVOTIONS

NOVEMBER 2

Jesus' best-known parable is "The Prodigal Son," a misleading title if ever there was one. The hero of this story is not the wandering boy but the waiting father! Jesus uses this parable to teach us about Father God's unconditional love, showing us that there is absolutely nothing we can do to make Him love us less—no sinful act, no degenerate deed, nothing. By the same token, there is nothing we can do to make God love us more. We are the objects of His love, but not the cause of it.

Psalms 103:10-12
"He does not treat us as our sins deserve or repay us according to our iniquities. For as high as the heavens are above the earth, so great is his love for those who fear him; as far as the east is from the west, so far has he removed our transgressions from us."

Lord Jesus, may I never abuse Your unconditional love. Help me to always walk in the light of obedience that I might fellowship with the Father. In Your holy name I pray. Amen.

ONE
MINUTE
D E V O T I O N S

NOVEMBER 3

Even though the people we pour our lives into may let us down, our acts of mercy are never wasted. Each act of love makes us more like Christ. Every act of faithful obedience is a worship gift we give to Jesus himself. And finally, every act of ministry is an expression of God's love—a word from Him as it were, expressing His great love and an invitation to return to Him.

2 Timothy 4:6-7
"For I am already being poured out like a drink offering, and the time has come for my departure. I have fought the good fight, I have finished the race, I have kept the faith."

Lord Jesus, teach me to pour out my life in ministry to others as an offering to You. In Your holy name I pray. Amen.

ONE MINUTE
DEVOTIONS

NOVEMBER 4

What small thing is the Lord asking of you today? Are you tempted to brush it aside as inconsequential, of no real concern? May I suggest you reconsider? Each act of obedience, no matter how small, prepares us for what God has for us in the future. If we don't take the small steps of obedience today, we will never be able to take the leap of faith when it is required of us.

1 Peter 4:10
"Each one should use whatever gift he has received to serve others, faithfully administering God's grace in its various forms."

Lord Jesus, help me to serve You in all ways great or small. In Your holy name I pray. Amen.

ONE MINUTE DEVOTIONS

NOVEMBER 5

I often tell aspiring writers that they will never finish a book if they strive for perfection, but if they don't strive for excellence, they will never publish one. Perfection is an unobtainable goal, imprisoning us in a cycle of repeated failure. Excellence is a shining star inspiring our best efforts and calling forth gifts we didn't even know we had. Avoid perfectionism like the plague, but strive for excellence with all your might.

Ecclesiastes 9:10
"Whatever your hand finds to do, do it with all your might."

Lord Jesus, I give You the work of my hands as an offering of love. In Your holy name I pray. Amen.

ONE MINUTE DEVOTIONS

NOVEMBER 6

One of the reasons we find it hard to truly listen to the doubts and fears being expressed by a friend or a spouse is that their painful concerns often reflect the very fears we have tried so hard to deny. Their anxieties threaten our carefully constructed denial system. The truth is, we can't allow others to process their painful doubts until we have faced our own doubts and fears and made peace with them.

Psalm 34:17,19
"The righteous cry out, and the LORD hears them; he delivers them from all their troubles. A righteous man may have many troubles, but the LORD delivers him from them all."

Lord Jesus, when the storms of life threaten and fear grips my heart teach me to honestly acknowledge my fear and bring it to You. In Your holy name I pray. Amen.

ONE MINUTE DEVOTIONS

NOVEMBER 7

If you are like most believers you struggle with guilt, both real and imagined. So how do we distinguish between true and false guilt? True guilt is conviction from the Holy Spirit and it draws us to God even as it convicts us of our sinful behaviors. False guilt is condemnation and it focuses on sins God has already forgiven. It always tempts us to despair, to give up, to turn our back on God.

2 Corinthians 7:10
"Godly sorrow [conviction] brings repentance that leads to salvation...but worldly sorrow [condemnation] brings death." (explanation mine)

Lord Jesus, deliver me from the lies of the enemy and free me from false guilt. In Your holy name we pray.

ONE MINUTE
DEVOTIONS

NOVEMBER 8

Guilt is one of the enemy's most effective weapons. He uses it to beat us down. But it is a lie. Unfortunately, many believers don't know how to distinguish between condemnation, which comes from the enemy, and conviction, which comes from the Holy Spirit. Conviction is always specific and it deals with a present situation. Condemnation is vague. It does not identify a specific sin; it simply makes us feel bad. Or if it does identify a specific sin, it is one from your past, one that has already been forgiven.

Romans 5:1
"Therefore, since we have been justified through faith, we have peace with God through our Lord Jesus Christ."

Lord Jesus, help me to embrace the conviction of the Holy Spirit even as I resist the condemnation of the enemy. In Your holy name I pray. Amen.

ONE MINUTE
DEVOTIONS

NOVEMBER 9

I once was caught in a blinding storm while fishing in the Gulf of Alaska. Without a compass or GPS we had no way of knowing whether we were heading out to sea or back to port. As far as we could tell we were totally alone. If the truth be known, it is quite likely that help was nearby. Only God knows how many well-equipped fishing trawlers passed just out of sight. So it is with life. When trouble comes it often blinds us to the help that is at hand. It feels like we are alone, abandoned by both God and man, but we are not.

Psalm 46:1
"God is our refuge and strength, an ever-present help in trouble."

Lord Jesus, help me to realize that You are near even when the storms of life blind me to Your presence. In Your holy name I pray. Amen.

ONE MINUTE DEVOTIONS

NOVEMBER 10

Sooner or later trouble comes to everyone. How you respond will determine your destiny. You can hug your hurts and make a shrine out of your sorrow, or you can offer them to God as a sacrifice of praise. If you can resist the temptation to blame God, you will discover that He is a very present help in the time of trouble and He will turn your mourning into dancing and restore the joy of your salvation.

John 16:33
"In this world you will have trouble. But take heart! I have overcome the world."

Lord Jesus, redeem my pain and disappointment. Use it to shape my character. In Your holy name I pray. Amen.

ONE MINUTE
DEVOTIONS

NOVEMBER 11

When trouble comes, the enemy will likely remind you of your past failures in an effort to convince you that you are getting what you deserve. You will face two dangers then. You will be tempted to recount every good thing you have ever done in a misguided attempt to prove you are a good person, or you will simply conclude that you are a bad person getting what you deserve. But there is a better way. Embrace God's love, even though you don't deserve it.

Hosea 2:23
"I will show my love to the one I called 'Not my loved one.' I will say to those called 'Not my people,' 'You are my people'; and they will say, 'You are my God.'"

Lord Jesus, help me to accept Your love even though I don't deserve it. In Your holy name I pray. Amen.

ONE MINUTE
DEVOTIONS

NOVEMBER 12

Some people mistakenly believe grace means God ignores sin, but nothing could be further from the truth. As Max Lucado writes, "God doesn't condone our sin, nor does he compromise his standard. He doesn't ignore our rebellion, nor does he relax his demands. Rather than dismiss our sin, he assumes our sin and, incredibly, sentences himself. God is still holy. Sin is still sin. And we are redeemed."

2 Corinthians 5:21
"God made him who had no sin to be sin for us, so that in him we might become the righteousness of God."

Lord Jesus, thank You for enduring the shame of the cross so that I do not have to bear the shame of my sins. In Your holy name I pray. Amen.

ONE
MINUTE
DEVOTIONS

NOVEMBER 13

When trouble strikes, the prayers and the presence of a trusted friend can be enormously encouraging. I don't understand all of the spiritual dynamics involved, but I know that something happens when we pray for each other. Our circumstances may not change immediately, but our burden is lighter. Somehow through the act of sharing our troubles and receiving the prayers of a special friend, God makes our heavy burden easier to bear.

1 Samuel 23:16
"Jonathan went to David at Horesh and helped him find strength in God."

Lord Jesus, I thank You for compassionate friends who have shared my troubles. Bless them I pray. Amen.

ONE MINUTE
DEVOTIONS

NOVEMBER 14

To walk by faith means to act on what we feel is God's direction, even though there is no way we can be absolutely sure that the voice we are following is God's voice and not our own. If we wait until we have resolved every doubt and answered every question, we will never do anything with our life. Go ahead, take a chance, step out in faith.

Hebrews 11:8
"By faith Abraham…obeyed and went, even though he did not know where he was going."

Lord Jesus, I truly want to do Your will. Give me the courage to follow You even when I don't know where I am going. In Your holy name I pray. Amen.

ONE MINUTE
DEVOTIONS

NOVEMBER 15

Embrace the gift of gratitude and you will discover the joy that eludes so many. The key is a thankful heart. You can complain about what you don't have and succumb to despair or you can learn to be thankful for what you do have and experience the peace of God that transcends all understanding. The choice is yours.

Philippians 4:6-7
"Do not be anxious about anything, but in everything, by prayer and petition, with thanksgiving, present your requests to God. And the peace of God, which transcends all understanding, will guard your hearts and your minds in Christ Jesus."

Lord Jesus, above all else I desire a thankful heart. Teach me to focus on my blessings rather than my needs. In Your holy name I pray. Amen.

ONE MINUTE DEVOTIONS

NOVEMBER 16

Maybe you have to be a grandparent to realize how neat kids are. Sometimes they're bundles of energy gift-wrapped in hand-me-downs. Other times they're pajamaed packages of sleepy sweetness. Always they're a miracle. I love the way they chase butterflies, and I love the attention they give to mud puddles and raindrops on a window. I envy their freedom from clocks and calendars, their immunity to pressure. Oh, they have their moments, skinned knees and naptime, but they recover quickly. They don't nurse their disappointments or make a career out of suffering.

Psalm 127:3 KJV
"Lo, children are an heritage of the LORD: and the fruit of the womb is his reward."

Lord Jesus, thank You for the miracle of life and the gift of children. In Your holy name I pray. Amen.

ONE MINUTE DEVOTIONS

NOVEMBER 17

Life on our troubled planet is often stormy and how we respond to its inevitable storms will determine the quality of our life and our destiny. The apostle's advice to his shipmates when they were caught in a life-threatening storm provides wise counsel for all of us. 1) Stay with the ship (Acts 27:31). 2) Get rid of all excess baggage (Acts 27:18,19,38). 3) Pray (Acts 27:29). 4) Don't lose heart. Keep up your courage (Acts 27:25). Remember, God is greater than any storm you will ever face.

Acts 27:25
"So keep up your courage, men, for I have faith in God that it will happen just as he told me."

Lord Jesus, give me courage to face whatever life brings and faith to believe that You will enable me to overcome every storm. In Your holy name I pray. Amen.

ONE MINUTE
DEVOTIONS

NOVEMBER 18

Justice is getting what you deserve. Mercy is not getting what you deserve. But grace is getting what you don't deserve. As sinners we all deserve eternal death, but God "...does not treat us as our sins deserve or repay us according to our iniquities. For as high as the heavens are above the earth, so great is his love for those who fear him; as far as the east is from the west, so far has he removed our transgressions from us" (Psalm 103:10-12).

Ephesians 2:8
"For it is by grace you have been saved, through faith—and this not from yourselves, it is the gift of God."

Lord Jesus, thank You for giving me what I do not deserve. May grace complete its holy work in me. In Your holy name I pray. Amen.

ONE MINUTE DEVOTIONS

NOVEMBER 19

Are you hurting right now? Has someone you loved and trusted sinned against you in unspeakable ways? Don't waste your pain. Ask God to use it to provide insight into yourself and into others. What does this experience say about you? What does it say about sin and temptation? How can you use it to become a stronger, more Christlike person? Give your pain to God and He will redeem it.

Psalm 138:7
"Though I walk in the midst of trouble, you preserve my life; you stretch out your hand against the anger of my foes, with your right hand you save me."

Lord Jesus, help me to make peace with my pain, to make it an ally instead of an enemy. In Your holy name I pray. Amen.

ONE MINUTE
DEVOTIONS

NOVEMBER 20

In a misguided attempt at self-improvement, we are often tempted to focus on our weaknesses when we should be focusing on our strengths. Determine right now that you are going to discover what you are good at and build on it. Don't try to be someone you are not. Don't copy someone else. Be yourself, but be the best self you can possibly be.

Romans 12:6
"We have different gifts, according to the grace given us."

Lord Jesus, thank You for the gifts You have given me. I can take no credit for them, but I am responsible for them. Help me to always use my gifts for Your glory. In Your holy name I pray. Amen.

ONE
MINUTE
DEVOTIONS

NOVEMBER 21

When David was preparing to fight Goliath, King Saul dressed him in a coat of armor and gave him a sword. David tried walking around in them but he soon realized they were a death trap. He wasn't Saul and he couldn't wear Saul's armor. The weapons he was skilled with weren't a sword or a spear, but a slingshot and a shepherd's staff and his faith in the name of the Lord! To be victorious, David had to be himself.

1 Samuel 17:45-46
"I come against you in the name of the LORD Almighty, the God of the armies of Israel, whom you have defied. This day the LORD will hand you over to me."

Lord Jesus, I am often tempted to emulate others more successful than myself in a misguided attempt to be someone I am not. Forgive us and help me to be who You have created me to be. In Your holy name I pray. Amen.

ONE MINUTE
DEVOTIONS

NOVEMBER 22

Sometimes I am tempted to think that all my praying and singing is wasted motion. I mean, I don't feel anything, I don't sense God's presence. But I press on—offering a sacrifice of praise, as it were—then suddenly everything changes and I realize all the effort was designed to press my face against the window of eternity until I could see Abba's face. True worship only happens when we catch sight of the Lord, high and lifted up.

Revelation 4:8,11
"Holy, holy, holy is the Lord God Almighty, who was, and is and is to come…You are worthy, our Lord and God, to receive glory and honor and power."

Lord Jesus, help me to worship by rote, if need be, until the revelation of Your presence turns my mechanical efforts into a spontaneous dance of praise. In Your holy name I pray. Amen.

ONE MINUTE
DEVOTIONS

NOVEMBER 23

Frequently we are angry at God because things haven't turned out the way we expected. As a result, we often find ourselves not only battling life's vicissitude, but we are also at odds with God himself. Some of us may even need to "forgive" God, not because He has done anything wrong, but because we have held Him responsible. When we "forgive" Him, we let go of those feelings—all of the hurt and anger, all of the bitterness and distrust. Once we get rid of those feelings, we can trust God again.

Hebrews 13:6,21
"So we say with confidence, 'The Lord is my helper...may he work in us what is pleasing to him, through Jesus Christ.'"

Lord Jesus, forgive me for harboring hurt and bitterness toward You. Restore my faith. In Your holy name I pray. Amen.

ONE MINUTE DEVOTIONS

NOVEMBER 24

Wouldn't it be great to be a kid again, at least for a day? To experience one more time the sheer joy of being alive, the pure pleasure of living one day at a time, fully savoring each moment. Of course that won't happen, but we can choose to have a childlike attitude. We will have to let go of past disappointments and the little hurts we've so carefully kept. And we will have to choose to embrace a childlike anticipation for life, a sense of wonder that makes each day new and life truly abundant.

Matthew 18:3
"And he said: 'I tell you the truth, unless you change and become like little children, you will never enter the kingdom of heaven.'"

Lord Jesus, I choose to become like a child in my joyous love for life. I choose to have a childlike faith. In Your holy name I pray. Amen.

ONE MINUTE
DEVOTIONS

NOVEMBER 25

We are conditioned to think our lives revolve around great moments. But great moments often catch us unaware—beautifully wrapped in what others may consider an ordinary moment. Like the time my wife was talking with an elderly lady in the Wal-Mart checkout line at Christmas time. Nervously the lady confided that she was afraid she didn't have enough money to pay for her groceries. When she began putting her items on the checkout counter, Brenda handed her credit card to the checker and told her to use it to pay for the lady's groceries. Now that was a small thing but it was a special moment!

Acts 20:35
"It is more blessed to give than to receive."

Lord Jesus, forgive me for missing opportunities like that. Make me more sensitive, more caring. In Your holy name I pray. Amen.

ONE MINUTE
DEVOTIONS

NOVEMBER 26

In a world beset with change, cultural evolution threatens the traditional family; still it remains the best connection we have with our personal past. From our family we get our identity, our personhood. Family traditions are the threads that link one generation to the next, giving us a sense of history and a place to belong. In times of crisis family provides a safe haven, a source of comfort in the dark hour of unspeakable loss.

2 Timothy 1:14
"Guard the good deposit that was entrusted to you – guard it with the help of the Holy Spirit who lives in us."

Lord Jesus, thank You for the spiritual values imparted to me by my family. Help my to pass them on to the next generation. In Your holy name I pray. Amen.

ONE MINUTE

DEVOTIONS

NOVEMBER 27

"After the Feast was over, while his parents were returning home, the boy Jesus stayed behind in Jerusalem, but they were unaware of it" (Luke 2:43). I think that describes many of us. We get so caught up in the day-to-day business of living that we lose touch with Jesus. We assume He is with us and are startled to discover that He's no longer a real part of our life. Or if He is with us, we pay Him no mind, thinking we know all there is to know about Him.

John 14:9
"Jesus answered: 'Don't you know me...even after I have been among you such a long time?'"

Lord Jesus, forgive me for taking You for granted. Help me to make You not only a part of my life, but the central part. In Your holy name I pray. Amen.

ONE MINUTE DEVOTIONS

NOVEMBER 28

Take a closer look at Jesus; take the time to really see Him. Notice things you've never paid any mind to—the way He gives His undivided attention to the person to whom He's speaking, no matter who they may be. Notice the way children flock around Him, how easily He's moved to tears by the suffering of others and how gentle He is toward those who have been battered and broken by life. In the end, I hope you find yourself loving Him in a way you've never loved Him before.

1 John 4:19
"We love because he first loved us."

Lord Jesus, help me to lay aside my preconceived notions and see You for who You really are—a friend of sinners. In Your holy name I pray. Amen.

ONE
MINUTE
DEVOTIONS

NOVEMBER 29

Jesus was a gregarious person whose name was at the top of every guest list. If He was present, the host need not worry; the party would be a success. His winsome smile and contagious laughter transcended all social barriers, turning a roomful of strangers into friends. Yet He was also a man of sorrows and acquainted with grief, and beneath His outgoing personality His heart ached, always ached, for those who were hurting. He carried humanity's pain in His heart even when He was enjoying a meal with friends, or laughing with children, or celebrating at a wedding.

Romans 12:15
"Rejoice with those who rejoice; mourn with those who mourn."

Lord Jesus, teach me to experience joy and sorrow simultaneously that I might live as an authentic human being. In Your holy name I pray. Amen.

ONE MINUTE DEVOTIONS

NOVEMBER 30

Jesus chose twelve disciples and they spent the next three years doing life together. They walked the same dusty paths, sweated under the same blistering sun. They ate the same meager fare and endured the same hardships. They disagreed, they argued and fought and made up. And all the while, the Holy Spirit was doing His work—turning them into a band of brothers who would risk their lives for each other, even die for each other.

John 15:13
"Greater love has no one than this, that he lay down his life for his friends."

Lord Jesus, help me to do life like that, so my friends and I might also be transformed into a band of brothers. In Your holy name I pray. Amen.

ONE MINUTE

DEVOTIONS

DECEMBER 1

My sister died when I was just nine years old. After the funeral we fled the house but we could not escape our grief. It filled the car as we drove through the December night looking at Christmas lights, trying to coax even a hint of joy out of a holiday season gone flat. It was my grief-stricken father's way of restoring our faith, his way of reminding us that what happened that first Christmas so long ago changed everything—even Carolyn's death. Now we had a new hope; the hope of being reunited with Carolyn in heaven.

Revelation 21:4
"He (God) will wipe every tear from their eyes. There will be no more death or mourning or crying or pain for the old order of things has passed away."

Lord Jesus, thank You for the promise of eternal life. May it give me hope no matter how dark the night. In Your holy name I pray. Amen.

ONE MINUTE
DEVOTIONS

DECEMBER 2

Although I have been blessed with many friends who have enriched my life, I also know the value of solitude. As a boy, I tramped the river bottoms in northeastern Colorado, both summer and winter. I fished and hunted, sometimes with friends, but more often alone. Early on I made friends with myself and learned to enjoy my own company. Others were not the source of my happiness, nor was I dependent on their approval. Only now, these many years later, do I appreciate how liberating that is.

Mark 1:35
"Very early in the morning, while it was still dark, Jesus got up, left the house and went off to a solitary place, where he prayed."

Lord Jesus, thank You for making me comfortable in my own skin. And thank You for the renewing gift of solitude. In Your holy name I pray. Amen.

ONE MINUTE DEVOTIONS

DECEMBER 3

John 3:16 does not say, "Whoever is free from sin shall be saved." No, it declares, "…whoever believes in him shall not perish but have eternal life." In other words, we are not saved because we have managed to remove all sin from our life but because we have believed in the Savior. Of course God's ultimate purpose is to deliver us from our sins, but what saves us is not the absence of personal sin but our relationship with the Savior.

Romans 10:13
"Everyone who calls on the name of the Lord will be saved."

Lord Jesus, I trust in You and You alone for my salvation. You are my only hope. Let me not be ashamed. In Your holy name I pray. Amen.

DECEMBER 4

For years I was an angry man and my anger always hovered just beneath the surface, causing my family to live with a fearful uncertainty. Yet even in my darkest moments, I hungered for the light of God's forgiveness. I desperately wanted to be different but I seemed powerless to change. Thankfully, God's grace has healed me and He can heal you too. That's the true meaning of Christmas. It reminds us of how wonderful life can be when the light of God's love comes spilling into our brokenness, making all things new.

Luke 1:46-47
"My soul glorifies the Lord and my spirit rejoices in God my Savior."

Lord Jesus, thank You for Your amazing grace that not only forgives my sins but also transforms my character. In Your holy name I pray. Amen.

ONE MINUTE DEVOTIONS

DECEMBER 5

As Christians, we must guard our hearts. Although we are called to stand for truth regardless of the cost, we must always walk humbly and in love. In the past we have spoken truth but without love and as a result, we have been perceived as being harsh and judgmental. In a misguided attempt to rectify this, some Christians now refuse to address the issues at all. Both extremes miss the mark. Truth without love can be harsh and judgmental, even as love without truth is permissive. But when we speak the truth in love it is transformational (see Ephesians 4:15).

Ephesians 4:29
"Do not let any unwholesome talk come out of your mouths, but only what is helpful for building others up."

Lord Jesus, forgive me for being arrogant and judgmental. Forgive me for being politically correct rather than truthful. Give me the courage to be both loving and honest. In Jesus' name I pray. Amen.

ONE MINUTE DEVOTIONS

DECEMBER 6

God does not love us because we are loveable, for if the truth be told, we are not all that loveable. Nor does He love us because we so desperately need to be loved, although we are, each and every one of us, desperate to be loved. God loves us because that is the kind of God He is. We are the objects of His love but we are not the cause of it.

Psalm 103:17
"But from everlasting to everlasting the LORD's love is with those who fear him, and his righteousness with their children's children—"

Lord Jesus, I don't know where I got the idea I had to earn Your love, but that wrong-headed thinking has nearly caused me to despair. I know I will never be good enough to earn Your love, so teach me simply to accept it. In Your holy name I pray. Amen.

ONE MINUTE
DEVOTIONS

DECEMBER 7

If God loves us unconditionally, and He does, that means there is nothing we can do that will make Him love us less—no foolish choice, no rebellious act, no sinful disobedience. By the same token, there is nothing we can do that will make Him love us more. If we could live a perfect life, please Him in everything we do, even die a martyr's death, He would not love us more because He already loves us absolutely, totally, and unconditionally!

John 3:16
"For God so loved the world that he gave his one and only Son, that whoever believes in him shall not perish but have eternal life."

Lord Jesus, teach me to trust Your love and to rest securely in it. In Your holy name I pray. Amen.

ONE MINUTE
DEVOTIONS

DECEMBER 8

The righteousness of Christ makes us perfect and refers to our justification or right-standing before God. Holiness refers to our daily walk, where the Holy Spirit is continually convicting us of sin and sanctifying us. If we are not being made holy by the continuing work of the Holy Spirit, one can only conclude that we have not been made perfect forever. Salvation is both instantaneous and continual. We are saved and we are being saved.

Hebrews 10:14
"Because by one sacrifice he (Jesus) has made perfect forever those who are being made holy."

Lord Jesus, I submit myself to the sanctifying work of the Holy Spirit. Make my daily walk a reflection of my right-standing before God. In Your holy name I pray. Amen.

ONE MINUTE DEVOTIONS

DECEMBER 9

The security of our salvation does not rest in what we do for Jesus, but in what He has done for us. He was made to be sin for us that we might be made the righteousness of God in Him (2 Corinthians 5:21). He became the Son of Man that we might become the sons of God. He bore the shame of the cross so that we need not bear the shame of our sin. He died that we might live!

Jude 24-25
"To him who is able to keep you from falling and to present you before his glorious presence without fault and with great joy – to the only God our Savior be glory, majesty power and authority, through Jesus Christ our Lord."

Lord Jesus, I have no confidence in the flesh. Left to my own efforts I will surely fail. You are my only security. I trust only in Your finished work. In Your holy name I pray. Amen.

ONE MINUTE
DEVOTIONS

DECEMBER 10

Having betrayed Jesus, Judas Iscariot discovered he could not live with himself. Frantically he tried to undo what he had done, flinging the thirty pieces of silver at the feet of the priests, but to no avail. Seeing he could not save Jesus, he went out and hung himself. If only he had realized that although it was too late for him to save Jesus, it was not too late for Jesus to save him. Betrayer though he was, he need not have died in his sin.

Matthew 12:31
"And so I tell you, every sin and blasphemy will be forgiven men, but the blasphemy against the Spirit will not be forgiven."

Lord Jesus, in my guilt I sometimes feel my sins are past forgiving. Deliver me from this deception and help me to receive Your love and grace. Forgive my sins. In Your holy name I pray. Amen.

ONE MINUTE DEVOTIONS

DECEMBER 11

Fill your mind with the Word of God and you will find yourself increasingly resistant to temptation. The Word of God will make you wise so you will not be taken in by the tricks of the enemy. The Word of God will make you pure so you will not desire the impure offerings of the world. The Word of God will transform you by the renewing of your mind.

Psalm 119:133
"Direct my footsteps according to your word; let no sin rule over me."

Lord Jesus, give me a burning desire for Your Word. In Your holy name I pray. Amen.

DECEMBER 12

There is no way to minimize the seriousness of sin. Whether we are talking about David's adultery, Peter's denial of Jesus, my anger, or some other sinful failure, we must never make light of sin. The wages of sin is always death (Romans 6:23). And if ever we are tempted to think that our sin is no big thing, all we have to do is take a look at the Cross. See Jesus bleeding and dying there, alone in the darkness, abandoned by God and man. That is what God thinks of sin. It must be punished.

Isaiah 53:6
"We all, like sheep, have gone astray, each of us has turned to his own way; and the Lord has laid on him the iniquity of us all."

Lord Jesus, thank You for suffering the punishment for my sin that I might be forgiven. Help me to ever live worthy of Your love. In Your holy name I pray. Amen.

ONE MINUTE
DEVOTIONS

DECEMBER 13

If you are serious about overcoming temptation, you will never deliberately put yourself in tempting situations. You will not flirt with danger! You will not overestimate your own spiritual strength, nor will you underestimate your propensity for sin. By realistically appraising both your strengths and your weaknesses, you will be able to live within your limits, thus minimizing the risks of yielding to temptation.

1 Corinthians 10:12
"So, if you think you are standing firm, be careful that you don't fall!"

Lord Jesus, help me to live circumspectly, fully appreciating the subtlety of temptation and the seriousness of sin. In Your holy name I pray. Amen.

ONE MINUTE DEVOTIONS

DECEMBER 14

In the heat of temptation we can think only of ourselves, only of the moment. The deceiver tells us to take control of our lives, to do it our way. He tells us to consider only ourselves, regardless of the consequences our actions may have. Once we buy into his way of thinking, there is almost no sinful choice that we cannot justify. Our "needs" take precedence over everything else—marriage vows, children, even God's law.

James 1:13-14
"When tempted, no one should say, 'God is tempting me.' For God cannot be tempted by evil, nor does he tempt anyone; but each one is tempted when, by his own evil desire, he is dragged away and enticed."

Lord Jesus, save me from my selfish self; deliver me from my preoccupation with self lest I fall into temptation and sin. In Your holy name I pray. Amen.

ONE MINUTE DEVOTIONS

DECEMBER 15

Prayer neutralizes the tempting lies of the enemy by refocusing our attention on God. In the secrecy of the imagination, where self is king, the beguiling suggestions of the deceiver are mesmerizing, even hypnotic. But when we enter the presence of God, we see them for the tawdry thing they really are. Prayer puts "this moment" of temptation into eternal perspective.

Matthew 26:41
"Watch and pray so that you will not fall into temptation. The spirit is willing, but the body is weak."

Lord Jesus, life has a way of crowding the eternal right out of my thinking. I become preoccupied with the here and now. Nothing matters but my immediate gratification. Teach me to pray, for only prayer can realign my life. In Your holy name I pray. Amen.

ONE MINUTE DEVOTIONS

DECEMBER 16

R Kent Hughes says, "Prayer is like a time exposure to God. Our souls function like photographic plates, and Christ's shining image is the light. The more we expose our lives to the white-hot sun of His righteous life (for say, five, ten, fifteen, thirty minutes, or an hour a day), the more His image will be burned into our character—His love, His compassion, His truth, His integrity, His humility."

2 Corinthians 3:18
"And we, who with unveiled faces all reflect the Lord's glory, are being transformed into his likeness with ever-increasing glory."

Lord Jesus, teach me to linger in prayer so that Your holy presence can do its work in me—conforming me to Your very own image. In Your holy name I pray. Amen.

ONE MINUTE
DEVOTIONS

DECEMBER 17

When choosing an accountability partner, you should select a person whose personal relationships are in good order. He should model the kinds of behaviors you seek to develop in your own life: faithfulness in the things of God, submission to godly authority, spiritual disciplines, trustworthiness, and self-control. He should also be well grounded in the Word of God. Since you will be sharing the most intimate details of your spiritual life, it is absolutely mandatory that your spiritual partner be a person of uncompromising integrity.

Titus 1:9
"He must hold firmly to the trustworthy message as it has been taught, so that he can encourage others by sound doctrine and refute those who oppose it."

Lord Jesus, give me the grace to live in community and to submit myself to spiritual overseers who will speak into my life. In Your holy name I pray. Amen.

ONE
MINUTE
D E V O T I O N S

DECEMBER 18

No accountability relationship is complete unless the covenant partners are committed to the spiritual disciplines, especially devotional reading and prayer. By committing to the same Bible reading schedule, you can encourage one another. By sharing many of the same books, you can have in-depth discussions that are mutually beneficial. You are also able to be more faithful in daily prayer because you know someone is holding you accountable.

2 Timothy 4:9,11
"Do your best to come to me quickly,...Only Luke is with me. Get Mark and bring him with you, because he is helpful to me in my ministry."

Lord Jesus, thank You for the godly people You placed in my life at critical times in my spiritual development. Help me to be that kind of spiritual friend. In Your holy name I pray. Amen.

ONE MINUTE DEVOTIONS

DECEMBER 19

The ultimate purpose of a covenant relationship is not accountability, but nurture. As a spiritual friend, your responsibility is not to make others "toe the line," but to enable them to become all God has called them to be. Spiritual friends are committed to protecting each other through mutual accountability, to be sure. Yet, if that becomes the sole reason or even the primary reason for the friendship, it will not long survive. The bread that nourishes the soul is acceptance and encouragement, not accountability.

Romans 16:3-4
"...Priscilla and Aquila, my fellow workers in Christ Jesus. They risked their lives for me."

Lord Jesus, I thank You for godly individuals who have laid down their lives to help me become the person You have called me to be. You know who they are, bless them I pray.

DECEMBER 20

God is at the very heart of Christmas, manifesting Himself in life's ordinariness. Even now He is revealing Himself through the birth of a child, the joy of common men, or in the toothless musing of an old priest. Remember, for those who pause to listen, the angels still sing, "Glory to God in the highest, and on earth peace, good will toward men."

Luke 2:19
"But Mary treasured up all these things and pondered them in her heart."

Lord Jesus, through the miracle of Your incarnation, You have made all of life sacred. Give me eyes to see You and a heart to worship You even when You reveal Yourself in the most unexpected ways. In Your holy name I pray. Amen.

ONE MINUTE
DEVOTIONS

DECEMBER 21

Pause for just a moment in your rush of holiday madness. Take a deep breath and let God grant you the true Christmas spirit—the genuine joy of spiritual worship, the wonder of angels singing, the excitement of shepherds stumbling through the dark in search of the Savior, the inspiration of Elizabeth's song, the spontaneity of Simeon's prophecy and the unmitigated joy of Anna's exclamation of praise!

Luke 2:14 KJV
Let us say with the angels, "Glory to God in the highest, and on earth peace, good will toward men."

Lord Jesus, help me to open my heart afresh to receive the gift of You this Christmas season. In Your holy name Ipray. Amen.

ONE MINUTE

DEVOTIONS

DECEMBER 22

When I think of Christmas, I think of the simple pleasure of family and friends, the excitement of children on Christmas morning, adult conversation laced with memories, childhood remembered and relived for a day. When I think of Christmas, I think of carols sung from the heart, true worship, candlelight communion, and prayer more real than words. When I think of Christmas, I think of Jesus giving us the gift of Himself.

Luke 2:11
"Today in the town of David a Savior has been born to you; he is Christ the Lord."

Lord Jesus, thank You for the gift of Yourself. May I always make room for You in my heart and in my overcrowded life. In Your holy name I pray. Amen.

ONE MINUTE
DEVOTIONS

DECEMBER 23

Christmas is a lot like life. It's full of contradictions and no little confusion. It's filled with both the good and the bad, with all of the generosity and all of the greed that is so characteristic of our fallen race. And as unlikely as it may seem, Jesus immersed Himself in our mess—He became one of us—in order to save us from our selfish selves. Now that's the true meaning of Christmas!

Matthew 1:21
"…And you are to give him the name Jesus, because he will save his people from their sins."

Lord Jesus, help me not to be distracted by the commercial glitz of Christmas, not to crowd You out. Help me to make room for You in my heart and in my life, this day and everyday. In Your holy name I pray. Amen.

ONE MINUTE DEVOTIONS

DECEMBER 24

Nothing can compare with the joy of giving. When I gave my wool overcoat to a homeless man on a bitterly cold December day, I thought my heart would burst, so great was my joy. That grateful man wrapped his arms around me and pulled me to his chest in a bear hug. He smelled like booze and body odor and damp clothes, but I didn't mind. His was the holiest hug I have ever received. In truth, it seemed as if God himself was hugging me.

Matthew 25:40
"Whatever you did for one of the least of these brothers of mine, you did for me."

Lord Jesus, thank You for allowing me to know the joy of giving. In Your holy name I pray. Amen.

ONE MINUTE
DEVOTIONS

DECEMBER 25

At least for one day each year, the world pauses in its mad busyness and our hearts turn toward home. Dim memories of our childhood faith tug at our hearts and we realize anew that we are truly spiritual beings, men and women made in the image of God. Within our hearts, hope burns eternal and on Christmas day all things are possible. Sins can be forgiven, broken relationships can be restored, and hurts can be healed. Best of all, we realize that God is with us.

Matthew 1:23
"'The virgin will be with child and will give birth to a son, and they will call him Immanuel' – which means, 'God with us.'"

Lord Jesus, may I always remember that You are the one who put Christmas in my heart and called me unto Yourself. In Your holy name I pray. Amen.

ONE MINUTE DEVOTIONS

DECEMBER 26

The abiding presence of God is always with us to strengthen and sustain us. The manifest presence of God comes to bless and deliver us. One is not better than the other, but they are different manifestations of God's great faithfulness. Be encouraged, God is with you this day and everyday.

Joshua 1:9
"Do not be terrified; do not be discouraged, for the LORD your God will be with you wherever you go."

Lord Jesus, I can do all things as long as You are with me. What I cannot bear is the thought of going it alone. Be very near to me all the days of my life. In Your holy name I pray. Amen.

ONE MINUTE DEVOTIONS

DECEMBER 27

Many of us live in a constant state of fatigue. We are tired, bone weary, from the inside out. A good night's sleep helps, but it cannot restore our spiritual and emotional energies unless it is supplemented by the inner disciplines of renewal—silence, solitude, and inwardness. Add to these the renewal generated by special friends, and you have a lifestyle that is continually replenishing the inner man. Truthfully, that's the only way we can remain fresh, given our hectic lives.

2 Corinthians 4:16
"Therefore we do not lose heart. Though outwardly we are wasting away, yet inwardly we are being renewed day by day."

Lord Jesus, renew me. Teach me to live within our limits, both physically and emotionally. In Your holy name I pray. Amen.

ONE MINUTE DEVOTIONS

DECEMBER 28

Joy is a many-splendored thing. It's special moments like births and baptisms, things that only happen once. It's your sixteenth birthday, turning twenty-one, landing your first job, buying your own car, and seeing the Grand Canyon for the first time. It's rare and tender moments—getting married and making love, giving birth, becoming a grandparent, growing old with the one you love. Joy is a many-splendored thing.

1 Thessalonians 5:16-18
"Be joyful always; pray continually; give thanks in all circumstances, for this is God's will for you in Christ Jesus."

Lord Jesus, help me to treasure all the special moments of my life. In Your holy name I pray. Amen.

ONE
MINUTE
DEVOTIONS

DECEMBER 29

Joy is a many-splendored thing—a strange and wonderful mixture of love and laughter, pain and sorrow, life and death. It's the comfort of friends when you stand beside the open grave of the one you've loved and lived with your whole life long. It's the strength of Scripture in the dark hour of unspeakable need. It's the memory of His faithfulness, the promise of His presence. Joy is a many-splendored thing.

2 Corinthians 7:6
"But God, who comforts the downcast, comforted us...."

Lord Jesus, I thank You for family and friends who have stood with me in the hour of our unspeakable need. Truly You have comforted me through them. Now make me a comfort to others. In Your holy name I pray. Amen.

ONE MINUTE
DEVOTIONS

DECEMBER 30

As we near the end of another year, I am thinking of all the things that bring me pleasure—a phone call from an old friend, a good book, a second cup of coffee, autumn colors, a warm fire on a winter night, the season's first snow, the sound of rain on a tin roof, the pungent odor of a dusty barn resurrecting childhood memories of haylofts and hide 'n seek. Gifts from God, each and every one.

James 1:17 KJV
"Every good gift and every perfect gift is from above, and cometh down from the Father."

James 1:17 KJV

Thank You, Lord Jesus, for all the joys of my life. Without Your abiding presence, they would have no meaning. Help me to never forget that. In Your holy name I pray. Amen.

ONE MINUTE DEVOTIONS

December 31

Life can be difficult at times. A beloved parent dies, you lose your job, your child gets in trouble, or a trusted friend lets you down. Disappointment sucks all the joy out of your life and depression dogs your days. Don't despair. God has a long history of speaking a word of hope in the darkness. When He speaks we have a choice. We can listen to His Word and act on it, or we can look at our circumstances.

2 Chronicles 20:15
"Do not be afraid or discouraged…For the battle is not yours, but God's."

Lord Jesus, as I come to the end of another year, give me hope. May I remember that You are greater than any difficulty I will ever face. In Your holy name I pray. Amen.

INDEX

Grief – January 31; March 28; July 27; August 1, 8; August 11, 15; September 6, 15, 16; October 2, 17; December 1

Grounded – May 11

Growing old – December 28

Growth – June 21

Guidance – January 1, 7; June 7, 23, 24, 25; September 12; October 9; November 14

Guilt – March 9; May 7; November 7; December 10

Happiness – December 2

Hardship – January 5; October 5

Harsh – December 5

Heal – April 1, 14; May 20; September 20

Healing – April 4; May 25; June 19, 21; August 17, 28; September 7, 8, 11, 19; October 28; December 25

Hearing – January 7; May 18

Heart – January 29; April 7; May 12, 22; September 9, 21; October 8, 24; December 25

Heart for God – March 8

Heaven – August 12; December 1

Help – January 5, 23, 31; April 20, 30; October 3

Heritage – March 22

Holiness – December 8

Holy – July 8, 9

Holy hugs – December 24

Holy Spirit – March 4; May 28; June 24, 26; October 24; November 30

Home – December 25